Tales from the Dales

To my granddaughters
Lisa and Jemma

Acknowledgement

My thanks to:

Mr and Mrs W. Trewhitt, Plump House
Mrs J. Spink, Thornton Watlass
Mr and Mrs R. Spink, Rookwith Grange
Mr and Mrs R. A. Corner, Cowling Manor
Also gratitude to Mrs Cole, Marton, for her valuable help.

FOREWORD

When Harry Andrew, a retired newspaper colleague of mine, telephoned one day in 1994 to say that his neighbour Dennis Chisholm had written an account of his life as a farmworker in Wensleydale, which Harry considered worth spotlighting in a newspaper article, I had little idea of the double pleasure that lay in store.

The first was meeting Dennis. Friendly and welcoming he also had that quiet, reflective manner that goes with the dalesman's intuitive habit of weighing things up carefully. Genuinely modest, he certainly had no thought of pushing his self-typed manuscript, which he stressed over and over again had been written for his family. 'Do you really think it is interesting?' he asked several times before I left.

But the manuscript was, of course, the second pleasure. From its intriguing first sentence, in which Dennis reveals he is unsure of his birthplace, it holds the attention. Dipping into it, I soon realised it was a vivid window on to what proved to be the last years of pre-intensive, pre-highly-mechanised farming. Dennis ploughed with horses, set up stooks of corn, raked the hayfields. When pacing out land for sowing he even used the now long-obsolete measures of rods, poles and perches he had been taught at school.

The Editor of the *Darlington and Stockton Times*, Malcolm Warne, shared my view that Dennis's manuscript was out of the ordinary. He not only allocated more than the usually-available space to my article about it but later, in response to keen reader interest, ran a second substantial piece based on it.

What made Dennis's manuscript, now this book, exceptional? The detail is what counts. Telling his story in an appealingly straightforward way, Dennis laces it with anecdotes that bring the past, and the characters he has known, richly to life. He shows a particular gift for writing in dialect – a difficult art. Read the remarks of farmer Richard Spink on his first train journey, in which 't'fost thing ah seed were a chetch run reet across a field', and the theory of a Bedale man about how the newfangled electric 'leet' had 'bunt' his lawn. This is social history – but entertaining with it.

Behind these cameos is a picture of dales life – indeed farm life everywhere – that has gone forever. Scanned from the perspective of today, when most farms are worked by just one or two men, the number of people on the land in Dennis's day was amazing. As he relates, he was one of eight people, including a full-time cook, on Richard Spink's farm at Thornton Watlass. When he and three companions cooled off in the Ure after a hot day's haymaking, they were just one of several groups from local farms bathing in the same short stretch of river. Though Dennis avoids introspection, could the loneliness of modern farm life be a factor in the worryingly high suicide rat among present-day farmers?

Showing typical kindness, Dennis allowed me to borrow the only copy of his manuscript to enable me to write my article. When I returned it I urged him to try and have it published. I am delighted that Pentland Press has now done so. Future historians of rural England will regard this little book as a nugget of pure gold. And any lover of the Yorkshire countryside, especially the Dales, who dips into it meanwhile, will come to much the same conclusion.

Harry Mead
Chief Feature Writer *The Northern Echo* 1969–1992.

I have tried to record my impressions of life from going to school when the sky seemed bluer, the grass greener, the summers longer, and the winters more endurable.

I suppose it's best to remember the good things in life, remembering the perfect summer's day with swallows chattering on the telephone wires, horse and cart going slowly by, cows eating contentedly on the village green, folk sitting out on chairs enjoying the evening sun, and the clang of quoits on the village green.

I have included dialect words which were in constant use as the spoken word then.

The day's work was long during the war years but I have not reflected on the times Richard Spink came to us when working and told us, 'Give over men, you have done plenty for today.' Work had to go on, never knowing when one had to be called out for Home Guard duties.

What a change from the end of the Second World War: now we have poverty caused by folk trying to keep up with today's luxuries, people still trying to keep up with their neighbours with motor cars and videos. Problems have changed, but have not ceased, today we have the perils of drug-taking and stealing.

F. D. CHISHOLM
1996.

I do not know in which village or where I was born on October 20th 1923. No church bells would ring out, nor cannons be fired. I would be born in what would be known as a hind house, my father being a farm worker like his father before him. There would be no going to hospital with all its modern equipment as happens today. My birth certificate shows, 'In the District of Northallerton'.

The earliest days that I can remember were at Stapleton, near Darlington. I started school at Cleasby at the age of five, being the second oldest in the family. Boys and girls from outlying farms walked to the village, then all together set off to walk the one mile to Cleasby. We had to walk through a stream which ran over the road, and was quite deep in winter. Strong boots with hob nails were worn when going to school, stockings which came up to the knee, short grey trousers, grey shirt, waistcoat, in which I carried cigarette cards, marbles being in my trouser pocket, jersey, top coat and cap. Some boys came to school with boots and leggings on in winter, girls had overshoes called galoshes, they generally carried a skipping rope to run with. You had not to be late for school or you had your knuckles rapped with a ruler; discipline was very strict, the head teacher being very expert with the cane.

The school was heated by a coke stove, a large kettle was placed on top to boil for making tea or cocoa when we had our sandwiches at dinner-time. While eating not a word had to be spoken, we had to sit quietly until everyone had finished. After the infants class there were standards 1-2-3 and 4. Pupils had to read out loud or monotonously chant the tables 7 x 3 are 21, etc. Slates were given out to write on, they were about 12" x 9" in a wooden frame. We wrote with a slate pencil and had to use a damp cloth to clean the slate. The girls used this while the boys used to spit on it then rub it off with their sleeves. If you were seen doing this your knuckles were rapped.

How well I remember coming home from school one day, mother being in bed and showing me a baby sister, the youngest in the family,

1

called Nancy. Many a time I had to rock the cradle, pulling on a string fastened to the cradle side. One day I gave it a good pull and the cradle fell onto its side. For this I got a good hiding from father, one of many, father being very strict.

School started each morning with a hymn, then scripture reading. Older boys and girls filled ink wells, distributed pens and exercise books for the day. When you had done writing, you had to sit up straight, no slouching or talking. No putting your pen or pencil in your mouth and chewing the end, it had to be put in the groove in the desk. These were long and seated up to six pupils, boys and girls mixed. When the vicar came into school the teacher had to say, 'Class,' everyone stood up, then all in chorus said, 'Good morning, Sir.' When meeting the teacher or vicar after school, you had to raise your hat or salute with the usual 'Good afternoon' or whatever.

A wood on the way to school was being felled off. We used to stand and watch them load the tree trunks onto the wood wagon, which stood under a 'three leg' (three telegraph poles standing on end and joined at the top). A wire rope from the top of the three leg was pulled by two horses to lift the tree trunk up to be loaded on to the wagon. When loaded, four horses pulled it away. The wagon was a long pole with wheels at each end, the back wheels were movable up and down the pole.

Farm stock going to market at Darlington used to be walked there on the Great North Road. This market is still held on a Monday. It was a regular sight to see sheep and cattle being driven on the roads.

One foggy Monday morning, as we were setting off to walk to school, beasts being driven on the road through Stapleton were run into by a charabanc. Three were killed, others had to be destroyed. I remember one being underneath the charabanc, as a bus was called then.

Sometimes we ran to school with our boolers. I remember a length of road made of stones rolled in, men breaking stones at the roadside to fill in holes before it was tarred and chippings put on. Steam engines were in use, a gang of men using big watering cans sprayed the tar onto the road from a tar-boiler which was pulled behind a steam engine, then men using shovels spread the chippings over it. Lastly, the big steam roller went over it making it smooth.

In the summer months tops and whips were used, cigarette cards were exchanged at play time.

One afternoon walking home from school, we came across a motorbike which had run into a horse and trap, the trap shaft was in the man's body. It was being sawn off by a man who lived near where it happened.

Sunday was the 'Lord's Day', we were never allowed to forget it. Chapel Sunday school was over the road. I can remember having to walk up some steps into a room above someone's house. When we came out of Sunday school it was, 'Go for a walk, keep yourself tidy, keep your shoes clean, no climbing walls, do not go down by the river or else!' We ended up walking down Strawgate Lane, finding snails in the wall, seeing who could find the best coloured one. Sunday afternoon we walked to Cleasby with the other children for chapel Sunday school, then to the church Sunday school. There was no getting out of going. We had two books each, the chapel one had a stamp put in it, the church one had a star stamped on it. By the time we had walked home it was time for tea. After tea it was over the road to the chapel evening service, then home to bed. We were never allowed to play with toys on Sunday as it was the 'Lord's Day'.

Our toys were very simple and provided us with hours of fun, with no television or wireless, only a wind up gramophone which mother used to put on for us. We had to amuse ourselves with playing games outside, such as, 'Sheep, sheep, come home', 'Poor Mary stands a-weeping', 'Cakes', 'Follow me to London', and many more.

November 11th, the whole school went to church for Armistice service, and the two minutes silence. In those days everyone stood for two minutes silence, cars, which were few, would stop, those working in the fields all stood in respect. Today, after two world wars they do not bother.

There were hard frosts in the winters when going to school, ponds froze deeper than today. Icicles a yard long would hang from the roofs of buildings. A pond down Boat Lane, Cleasby, was popular for sliding on. One dinner hour when we were sliding the ice gave way, a boy fell in, the big boys pulled him out as the men who worked at the farm nearby were returning for work. One man 'boxed' the boy's ears, gave him a good telling off, then his father came and he kicked the boy's behind all the way back to their house. Today the teacher cannot give the cane, spare the rod and spoil the child. Boat Lane went down to the river Tees, here there was a crossing for horses and carts, we used to see them crossing when we were out on a nature walk, this was a short cut to Darlington.

In the living-room of our house there was an open fire for warmth, pans were put on to boil, a side boiler provided hot water, a double burner paraffin lamp stood on a table in the back kitchen which we called a 'Kelly lamp'. If this got bumped, it just rocked and stayed upright. In winter when the nights were cold and frosty, we used to take a warm brick inside an old sock to bed. We had our own bricks – through the day they were left in the side oven, they were always lovely and warm. We were never allowed to light candles, play with matches, poke the fire or get hot water out of the side boiler. We had to be in bed by 7 o'clock each night after having cocoa with jam and bread for supper.

With father working on the farm, I used to go with him for a ride in the cart. Once, when father was loading gravel by hand from the bed of the River Tees, I was walking around when I came across a dead man in some willows. He was a fisherman who had been caught by a flash flood. His body was put into a long box by two men, then placed in father's cart and taken to the public house in the village.

One Saturday afternoon when father was coming into the village from ploughing with his two horses, I dashed to tell him I had just seen a man run out of the village pub on fire. The man, Eric Manners, then ran from the back of the pub onto the road, a man passing on a bicycle jumped off and rolled him in the snow on the green. By then smoke and flames were pouring from the window, where a paraffin lamp had exploded. At first father would not believe me, until he saw smoke and flames coming out of the broken window. Tying the two horses to the farm yard gate, he ran across to help.

The school was closed for one day, for the funeral of the head teacher's mother, so I went with father to Darlington for a load of coal, enjoying the ride in the cart. On our return we met the horse-drawn funeral coming towards us. All the horses were black. Father stopped the horse and cart and stood with bowed head, cap in hand, while the cortege passed by on its way to Croft church. After it had passed by I got a good telling off and a clip over the ear for not taking off my cap to show respect for the dead. I would be eight years old then.

At school a 'gob stopper' was handed round, one sucked a colour off then gave it to the next boy. For half a penny you could get two gob stoppers, that is really the only sweet I can remember. It was out of the question asking for a penny for sweets. How well I remember one Christmas having a tin road-roller. It was small but when wound up it went forward and then back. The boy next door had one much bigger, but because it would not go backwards he stood on it and broke it. I would willingly have exchanged with him.

A gate between the houses lead onto a cart track which went down to the River Tees, where the gravel was being taken out. We lived in the house on the left for a while. A church service was held in the front room each month. I was told to keep quiet while the service was going on. If you look you can still see the outline of the church window. I last saw it in 1988, it had been half bricked up, the coloured window gone.

Playing up a plum tree in our back garden one day I heard a roar. It was a wall of water crashing down the River Tees. From my vantage point I had a good view, men who were getting the gravel out began to shout as they ran up a gantry for safety. They had no time to release the horses from the gravel tubs. Some were swept away and drowned, their carcasses being recovered near Croft. During a thunderstorm one day, a ball of light came down and floated about before touching the ground. What a crack it made, frightening two horses eating grass on the village green, and they bolted out of the village.

Water for drinking and for wash days had to be carried from the village pump, this being at our side of the road. Water for washing days had to be boiled on the open fire in a large pan, we had no copper fire. Puddings were always boiled, such as 'spotted dick' and jam puddings. Mother did all the baking of bread and pies in the side oven. Pies were made of whatever fruit was in season, such as plums, apples and blackberries. We were only given cake for tea on Sundays.

Uncle Ken lived in Stapleton, the house he lived in had a floor of earth, as did a house lower down where the Misses Wilson lived. Each house had an earth closet which was down the back garden, they had an ash pit behind so that household waste and ash from the fires could be mixed together.

The family left Stapleton on the 13th May 1933, and moved to a village called Finghall in Wensleydale. Father was to be hind for Mr Kirk. Father's wage then was £1-10-0 a week with free house, milk and potatoes. For this father had to start work at 6 o'clock in the morning, to have the milk at the station to catch the milk train at 7.30 each morning, then milk each night after 5 o'clock, coming home between 6.30 and 7 p.m., seven days a week. I do not remember father having any holiday.

School then was at Constable Burton, two miles over the fields, we had no transport. To walk by road was three miles, going by way of Hutton Hang and Constable Burton station. The beck which passed through Constable Burton had a working mill lower down and when we walked to school over the fields we passed the mill. The big water wheel was turning, horses and carts brought sacks of corn to be ground, others were being loaded up. The winter of 1933-4 was very severe, with keen frosts and deep snow. Going to school I came across my first snowdrift, soon my boots were wet, they had to stay damp all day, the coke burning stove had a guard round so that we were able to put our wet coats and caps to dry.

In the fields in summer, bird life was plentiful, such as woodcock, jay, snipe, plovers and water hens nesting on the beck side. One farm we passed when going to school was farmed by Singletons, they all wore clogs, even the two daughters. They gave us apples and plums to take home, especially after a big wind.

In spring, I went with father when he was rowing up for potatoes and turnips. I would remove eggs out of plover nests, then replace them after the row had been made. The plovers sat until the last minute, they were not afraid of the horses. Mr Kirk went round the sheep in a tub trap, I used to have a ride with him, he also took the 'lowence' out in the trap.

After my 11th birthday in October 1934, father took ill. He had to go to hospital at Darlington, where he died two weeks later, on November 5th. Mother was left with five children to look after on a widow's pension of 10/- a week (50 pence).

Bill Harker, a single man in the village, went to work for Mr Kirk, mother took father's place milking the cows, morning and night, seven days a week, until we could find somewhere to live. I gave mother a hand with the cows and feeding the calves.

Mr Kirk was a kind man who went to chapel. Sunday nights the chapel was full, those from the outlying farms came by horse and trap, the horses were left in Mr Kirk's farm yard. All the men sported a buttonhole of sweet pea, or whatever was in flower. Two men who came to chapel used to stamp their feet and shout, 'Amen. Praise the Lord!'

Anniversary and Harvest Festival Sundays were big events when folk came from other villages such as Thirn and Newton-le-Willows.

Things took a turn for the worse after father died, regarding both food and clothing. Mother received no money for milking, but was allowed to stay in the house rent free. George Harker had a son called Clarence working on the farm, his byname was 'Gadge'. I soon found out when I was with Gadge that I got good food, both at his mother's and other farms where we went to give a hand with the hay or harvest. Mr Harker had a trap which he used for going to Bedale and Leyburn markets, also for going to chapel in other villages. I used to help wash and polish the trap, then cover it over with a stack sheet to keep the hens off. All the horse brass had to be cleaned and polished before going to market.

Mrs Harker reared chickens, 'clockers' sat on the eggs which were under coops. Before the 'clockers' were put under the coops for sitting, a sod was cut out of the ground with a spit, this made a circular hole, then chaff was put in the bottom for the sitting of eggs. A wire mesh cage which the clockers fed under had to be pulled in front of each coop. While the clockers were feeding, the eggs were turned then a little warm water sprinkled over them. This was done by dipping your fingers in the ladling can of warm water, then flicking it over the eggs. A dozen coops were behind a wall, fresh water was to carry each day. Each coop had a door in front to keep it dark for the clockers, rats tried to scratch under the coops, crows and magpies hung around.

When the chapel Sunday school went to Redcar by train from Finghall station, what excitement there was! This was the first time our family had been away together. Gadge gave me sixpence, I had never had so much money to spend. The train had children on from up the dales. It stopped at other stations to pick children up, it must have been a special train for the day.

Quoits were played near the blacksmith's shop on the village green, they seemed to ring and clang all night, along with the hammering of the blacksmith. It was here that I saw the blacksmith and his man putting new rims onto cart wheels. The wheels were made fast onto a round stone, like a mill stone with a hole in the middle where the hub was made fast with a steel shaft. The new iron hoops or rims were made hot in a bonfire on the green, then placed on the wheel which caught fire. When hammering the rim on, cold water was thrown over it and nails made by the blacksmith were used to secure the rim onto the wheel.

Men gathered in the blacksmith's shop to talk. On one such occasion a smallholder called Widser Lockey said, 'Nobody will ever get my rabbits.' He forgot who was listening. Gadge said, 'Didter hear that farmer? We'll 'ev 'em.' I was fitted out with a top coat called the 'poacher's coat' to cover a piece of 'billy band' which went round my waist. Each Sunday afternoon with Spot his dog – which was almost human – rabbits were got out of Widser's field. They were carried past his house under the 'poacher's coat', four at a time. This was pocket money for Gadge and myself, rabbits then would be 1/6d a couple. (7½p.)

When I was eleven years old, at haytime, I was able to use the horse and rake to clean rake the hayfields, while the men were busy making hay pikes. The hay was samed up with a paddy sweep. It took three sweep loads to make a pike and they were made in rows across the field. A pike bogey was used when taking them to the barn in the stackyard. When a hay stack was being made in the field, a chain was put round them, two horses pulled it to the stack. Lots of beer was drunk by the men, ginger beer for the women and children.

EAST WITTON 1935

The family left Finghall in August 1935, moving into a stone-built cottage, number 30, which belonged to Jervaulx Estate, known locally as 'Jervo'. The rent was 1/6d per week, which was paid twice a year at the Blue Lion Inn, November 11th (Martinmas), then May Day, 13th May.

How different East Witton was to the other villages with its large village green, houses all round it, nestling under Witton Fell. Men and women wore clogs, horses were on the green to keep the grass short, three taps for drinking water stood on the green and there were two shops and a butcher's shop. The blacksmith's shop had been made into the Village Institute. Two quoits pitches on the green were well used, there was a Reading Room for the young men.

I soon found out on going to school that we were the odd ones out, that more than half the school was related to one another, even those from the outlying farms. Forty children attended school then. Once accepted I soon made some good friends. It was Ron Baddon who asked if I would go potato picking in the October at Danby Lodge, near where he lived. Ron's parents lent me a bicycle for the week to ride home on. This was the first time that I had picked potatoes for money. Each one had a length to pick which was marked out with sticks, 15 yards for the older boys, less for the younger ones. Starting time was 8 o'clock until 5 o'clock, Saturday afternoon 4 o'clock. For this week's work I received 5/- (25 pence) which went to buy new boots for the winter.

Ron Baddon was related to Nat Hutchinson the butcher's son. Each Monday morning a bullock was pulled down to the ring for killing. This was always done before school started. The rope was passed out over the lower half of the door and all the boys pulled on it until the nose of the bullock was against the ring in the middle of the floor. Then Joe, Nat's brother, held a felling axe in the middle of its head, his father then hit it with a wooden mallet, then it was off to school.

The first winter at East Witton was very bad for snow. The school was closed, the snow was knee deep. I had never seen so much snow. My school pal, Archie Kirby, and I were helping to dig snow from house fronts onto the road, then to the village taps; we carried water for old people. When the snow plough did come round the village it was pulled by four horses. It was so cold that the dish cloth used to freeze hard onto the stone sink inside our house, the windows had flower patterns on with the frost.

When spring was coming, curlews and plovers came onto the fields down by the River Cover before going onto the fell top. It was their arrival that made spring more welcome after all the cold days. Rabbits ran about in thousands, the fell-side and fields down by the River Cover stank of them. When mother wanted a rabbit for a pie, Archie and I used to get one out of the stone walls, then replace the stones so as not to leave a hole; we were able to take our pick of rabbits.

Mother got a job working at Jervo for Christie's, who owned Jervaulx Estate, three days a week at 2/6d per day, i.e. 7/6d or 37½ pence per week which made things better for the family. At the same time, Mrs Dinsdale asked if I could go to milk for her each Friday night, because Bill her husband always came home 'market fresh' from Leyburn market. Four o'clock I had to go for tea, then, carrying a back can or kit, Mrs Dinsdale with two pails on a yoke, we set off to walk out at the top end of the village, through a stee (stile) down a long field to the laith (barn) where six cows were brought in to milk. The back can which I carried would hold five gallons. Mrs Dinsdale carried milk in the two pails using the yoke, she also wore clogs. When back at the farm house, the milk had to be separated, the 'blue blob' as it was called, was fed to the calves, the cream later made into butter which was taken to Leyburn market in a butter basket. Many a time I have helped to churn for butter.When the weather was hot and thundery, water was used from Peacock's well because it was very cold. Mrs Dinsdale used flat wooden patters she called 'Scotch hands'. She was able to make a pound of butter with very little to add or take off. This was done after the butter had been clashed, weigh bogeys were used for weighing the butter. My last job then was to use a roller on each pound to imprint a thistle which was Mrs Dinsdale's trademark. For this I received 6d, 2½p a pound of butter and a jug of buttermilk for mother to bake with.

SUNDAY – EAST WITTON

Sunday morning, three horses grazed on the village green, all was peaceful. A clocker with chicks came out of Tot Shield's yard to scratch in the roadside gravel in front of our house. Cows were turned onto the green, they belonged to Tot Shield. After a while they were taken out at the top end of the village up Braithwaite Lane into his field. Tom Hutchinson, the butcher, turned his cows onto the green. After a while they were taken out at the bottom end, down Cover Bridge road to a small meadow field, where corn crakes nest in summer; it was full of wild flowers.

Matt Wells would be busy pulling his home-made hand cart, with two small milk cans on, these were back cans or kits, which held seven gallons each. He called at each house as he went round the village selling

The Butcher turns his cows onto the green.

his milk. The milk was warm, having just been through a sile to take the dirt out. It was taken from the can with a pint measure to put into the jug. Mother got good measure from Matt.

After putting on my Sunday clothes, I called for my school pal Archie Kirby, then it was off to chapel Sunday school. As we came out of chapel, the church bells would start to ring as we walked down the village into the church vestry. There we put on a cassock and surplice then walked down the aisle singing the first hymn with the choir and the bell ringers who had now joined us. Church was well attended. Only two cars stood in front of the Blue Lion pub, they belonged to Christie, the Estate owner and Mr Maughan, the Estate Agent. Shops were closed. If one had to call at the back door of Mrs Poulter, the shop owner, what a ticking off you got, Sunday was a day of rest – GOD'S DAY, you were never allowed to forget it.

Afternoon it was church Sunday school, no games were played on a Sunday, the Reading Room was closed, young men gathered at the bottom end of the village behind the Institute to talk, a good crowd, all in their Sunday best with a buttonhole of flowers. When it was time for church and chapel evensong, each went to their own place of worship. Church was well attended on a Sunday night. Only essential water had to be carried from the village taps. Walking over the fields to the River Cover, or up the fell when warm was a pastime in summer.

At about 4.30 p.m., Tot Shields would be setting off with a pail of hen corn to feed the hens, which were in the same field as the cows. He would then bring the cows back home with him for milking. A horse and trap with Mr Harrison in went up the village to Mr Thwaite's house. He would be the local preacher for Sunday night. After having tea with them, he came to preach at the chapel. 'Hell and Damnation', Eternal punishment, would put the fear of God into us children. One anniversary I well remember him looking at us from the pulpit, then getting very excited with himself. (First you must know that the words 'arse end' were well used, such as the arse end of the cart, meaning back end of, and that a pike was a small stack of hay. When pulled away to the stack, it left a round, yellow ring where it had been stood.) Mr Harrison looked down on us and shouted, 'Now all you young lads and lasses, I want you to make a mark in life, a mark in life, a mark as big as a pike's arse!'

One local preacher from Scrafton told us about walking on the moor top, when, he said, 'I saw I was walking on God's flowers (heather) so Ah sent dog yam, then knelt down ti pray, ti ask God's forgiveness for stannin on his flowers, then tip-toed off yam.'

Another one from Coverdale was telling us about going to the laith (stone barn) one Sunday morning and finding it full of rabbits. 'Did we kill those rabbits, my friends? No, we fastened them in, then killed them on the Monday morning.'

Mrs Airy from Middleham used to pray for all the rabbits that were going to be cut with the grass cutters and binders. In those days there were rabbits in millions running about.

Mr Harrison from Harmby used to tell us his life story in dialect, that was the spoken word then. 'Me fatha and I were on t' stone heap breaking stones, when someone said, "Fancy auld Harrison brekkin steeans fer a livin!" Me fatha jumped up off't steean heap saying, "Div I owe thee owt, if Ah dee Ah'll pay thee now." He was stanin theer wi his poss (purse) in his hand. Now, there's a man if ever there was one, me fatha.'

Sunshine Corner was held every week in the chapel. In winter months lantern slides were shown, which were generally about Africa. I had to attend a meeting in the chapel called S.P.C.G – Society for the Propagation of the Christian Gospel. Choir practice was at church every Friday night for one hour. In 1936 when I was 13 years old, I took over blowing the church organ. For this I received 11/6d – 57½ pence a year, which included blowing the organ for weddings and funerals.

When a funeral took place while I attended school, after the church service I had the rest of the day off school, children then never went to a funeral. A bier for carrying the coffin on was taken round the village pulled by the bearers. As it passed the houses they came out to walk behind the coffin, all were dressed in black, curtains were drawn across the windows.

I remember singing round the piano at Mrs Thwaite's house practising for the Sunday school anniversary after the S.P.C.G. meetings. Sunshine Corner, Sunday school, choir practice, one got fed up, but you had to go.

The vicar, Revd. A.P. Durrant, came into school each morning to say prayers before lessons started. One morning he asked if I would go and pump the organ. A man from Leeds was coming to clean and repair the organ. This took three days, he stayed at the Blue Lion Inn. We only had candlelight to work with, most of the work he did was at the back of the organ where it was very narrow. The reeds were taken off and cleaned. This man stuttered when talking to me, and when working in the narrow passage, he kept blowing out the candle, which meant we were more in the dark than candlelight. I used nearly a box of matches.

From the newspaper 50 years ago: Hundreds of mice are proving a plague inside the valuable organ of St John's Church, East Witton. Not only do the mice play hide and seek and nest in the inner workings of the instrument, but they boldly come out during church services, to the annoyance of the Vicar, (Rev. A. P. Durrant, M.A.), to the amusement of the choir, and the amazement of the congregation. Fortunately, the organist, Miss Aydon, is not nervous about these numerous creatures, which have caused the pedals to be inoperative and have generally interfered with the working parts of an instrument which Dr. Moody, organist of Ripon Cathedral, ranks highly among church organs. The infestation of the church by mice was the chief subject at the recent Easter vestry meeting, where the Vicar read a letter from organ specialists (Messrs. Binns, Fitton and Haley, of Bramley, Leeds), stating that the mice had done considerable damage to the organ. They submitted an estimate of £52 10s to overhaul the organ.

Jack Ryder and Nobby Clark were length men working for the North Riding County Council. They cut the roadside grass by hand in October, then after cleaning it up, they left the heaps for the village bonfire on November 5th. The butcher's flat cart was used for gathering up the grass and leaves. We pulled the flat cart by hand – Tom Poulter, Eric Robinson, Ron Baddon, Nipper Harrison, Tedding Fielding, myself and Archie Kirby. The local farmers brought their hedge cuttings. This was the largest village bonfire that I had seen. November 4th, we went round the village shouting, also carrying the school hand bell.

'Remember, remember, the 5th of November
Is gunpowder, treason and plot.
Do you see any reason why gunpowder treason
Should never be forgot?

So all the boys, all the boys, let the bell ring.
Please will you give something for the bonfire'.

Each house would give a few coppers, which were shared out among those who had been helping with the bonfire. The most that I can remember receiving was 8d, which went on a few fireworks, such as squibs and sparklers. A boy called Les Plant was hit in the face when throwing fireworks about. He lost an eye, there was no more throwing of fireworks after that.

Dark winter nights we usually played 'Jacky, Jacky, show your light', which was good fun. One game we played when there was no moon and it was windy was 'pin and button'. A length of black cotton was fastened to a button, sometimes two, which was then pinned to the corner of a window pane, cotton on the reel was then fastened to the cotton from the button, then taken across the road onto the green, where we laid flat on the grass to pull on the cotton, which made the button tap the window pane until they came out to see what it was, then we started again after they had closed the door. Dark, wet nights were spent in different houses playing draughts, snakes and ladders or card games. Christmas time we played pulling the parcel, a shoe box all nicely wrapped up with a long length of string fastened to it, when dark it was placed on someone's step, knock on the door, when they bent down to pick it up it was pulled across the road.

On Hallowe'en night candles were used inside turnips which had been scooped out, then eyes and a mouth were cut in. A candle inside a jam jar was used when going for water to the village tap when dark, some had small stable lamps. Some nights were very still, pitch dark, and eerie, especially when the screech owls were calling out. Church clocks and train whistles would be heard from miles away. Conkers were well played at school from October. They had a hole made in them with a nail, were placed in the side oven to make them hard, then they were threaded on to string. We used to walk over the fields to the River Cover, then go over the stepping stones to Middleham where there was a picture house; for 2d I remember seeing Laurel and Hardy, also Will Hay. Hair cut at Middleham cost 2d for short back and sides.

'Bags I Piesy'

When playing rounders at school, or summer nights on the village green, one would shout out, 'Bags I Piesy', meaning that they wanted to be first at throwing the ball. The ball was always 'chucked', never thrown under hand, the ball was then hit by hand. We never used a bat or stick. Coats and caps from the boys were used as corners to run to.

French cricket would be played as well. This was played with a bat, no wickets, the one using the bat had to stand still, only twist his/her body. The ball had to be bowled under hand at the feet, the idea was for the ball to touch the shoe, then you were out. Wherever the ball came to rest after being hit with the bat, the fielder had to bool from there. It was up to the one with the bat to try and keep the ball in front of them.

Once, when playing cricket on the green, a ball went over the roof of Waxy Jacksy's house, we never got the ball back. He lived with his sister Arabella. They were never seen out in the village, two very odd people. They used to walk the four miles to Leyburn market with a basket of eggs, then walk home again.

Nat, the butcher's son, had to wear a brace to keep his back straight, he was not able to run and had to walk with a stick. Nat loved cricket. When he was batting I was his runner, this was all right on the village green, but when it came to playing another school at Cover Bridge it always caused trouble. I would be down the wicket and back before the other batsman had turned round. Many a time fighting broke out after a match with the other school arguing over his runner. Don't forget that most of those playing for East Witton school were related to Nat.

East Witton had a sports day. If you had no money you really ran your best for the prizes. My last sports day before leaving school was in the summer of 1937. That day I made 4/-, (20 pence), giving mother 3/6d. First prize in a race was 6d, (2½ pence) to win the fell race was 2/6d, I was never lucky enough to win that. That same summer the church trip went to Redcar, despite little spending money it was an exciting time for us all. Little did I know that it would be the last day away for many years.

In that same summer of 1937 there was a violent thunderstorm, the two rivers became as one. Cover Bridge Inn was flooded, the flood water came across the road halfway between East Witton and Cover Bridge, bursting the River Ure bank near Jervaulx causing vast flooding, washing sheep away, rabbits in thousands were drowned. With the land being so hard and dry, water ran down the fell-side like a huge sheet of glass, flooding the lower fields.

During that hot summer holiday, we used to walk down to the River Cover, each carrying a few sandwiches and a bottle of home made lemonade. The place we went to was all flat rocks; after splodging around, and trying to swim, we used to lie out on the warm rocks to dry off.

Dick Stott from Cover Bridge used to take lunch for the grouse shooters on top of Witton Fell. When at school it was Bill Croft, whose parents farmed at Tranmire, who told us that a plane was coming to pick up some grouse. After school we set off to walk to Tranmire farm above Witton Fell, arriving in time to see a light, single engine plane land in one of their meadows. After loading the grouse it soon took off. The plane was all red with white lettering on.

Old Hilda Metcalfe did washing for other people, such as farmers or anyone who was ill. For 2/6d (12½ pence) Hilda took her pram for the washing, washed and ironed it, then took it back. For some reason a man was staying with Hilda. After a while it got around the village that he was demanding money from her, then that he was hitting her. I well remember the vicar going to tell him off, but to no good. The young men in the village, Jeff, Kelly, Shavings, Jimmy Foy, were determined to get rid of him. One night, when it was dark around 7 o'clock, I was lifted onto the back kitchen roof with a wet coal sack. After walking up to the chimney, I placed the wet sack over it to smoke him out. I was told to stay there until he came out, then remove the sack. He came out coughing, they gave him a good hiding and told him to be going or he would get some more. I was able to jump off the low roof after witnessing this. This took place at the back-end of 1936.

The previous winter of 1935-6, we were out playing on the green one dark night when we became aware of a very bright light at the top end of East Witton up Braithwaite Lane. It suddenly went out, then came on again, then vanished. As a rule we were indoors by 7 o'clock. The next night we stayed out and saw the light shining again in the same place. Kirby and I set off to walk towards it, we had never seen such a bright light. When we reached Pickard's farm all the trees and sheep in the fields were clearly seen, just like daylight. The light seemed to be at Coverham and, as before, it went out, came on again then vanished, what it was we did not know. When talking to older folk who had never seen it, they all said it would be a flare from Catterick Camp, but a flare always comes to earth, not this light.

Another sight we saw when out playing on the green one winter's night, was the Northern Lights. What beautiful colours reached up into the sky. I well remember being frightened, so Kirby and I ran into his house to tell his father, who explained what it was.

The stone built cottage we lived in was snug and warm in winter when mother had a nice bright fire. A twin wick oil lamp with a glass bowl stood on the table to give light, while Joyce, Nancy and I played card games, mother would be sewing while listening to the wireless. The wireless had an accumulator, this lasted about one month. A man from Middleham came round with fully charged ones, and exchanged them for 6d. He came with a pony and trap and would also take shoes to be repaired.

The range in the kitchen had a right hand oven with a side boiler on the left. The oven was kept white inside, while the outside was blackleaded each Friday. A reckan and crane went from left to right and moved up and down. This was for the cast iron pans and kettle to hang from. A piece of iron called a 'Dog' had to be placed against the oven to stop the fire going under when not in use. The flues had to be cleaned out regularly, soot scraped from the chimney as far up as one could reach with the cowl rake. A 'Tidy Betty' stood in front of the fire to keep the ash from falling too far out. The fender was rubbed with a damp cloth dipped in the fine ash from under the fire to keep it bright. The hearth was made white with a donkey stone, all ashes were to riddle, the dust went into the ash pit. It was my job to see that coal and logs were brought in for the night and kindling sticks to light the fire next morning.

I had to run down to the shop with a stone jar to be filled with black treacle which came out of a wooden barrel, there was no such thing as Golden Syrup. Paraffin was carried from the shop in a can with a hinged lid on and a spout, this cost 6d a gallon. Candles were 2d a packet. Matt Wells brought coal round the village with his horse and flat cart, one hundredweight of coal cost 10d.

Petrol cans which held two gallons and marked ESSO or PRATTS were strapped onto the running board of motor cars. Farthings were in general use, they would buy one gob stopper. Myrtle Hall took the daily paper round the village, the *Northern Echo* cost one penny. Newspapers were never thrown away, each page had to be folded, then cut with a knife into squares, then hung up in the 'Nessy'. A lot of nessies had a double seat, one for a child.

Potato peelings and cabbage leaves were taken to the nearest person keeping a pig to kill. A wooden barrel stood outside where the pig was kept, this was called pig swill. How well I remember the smell of sour milk with all the flies round the barrel.

Haytime started around the end of June, then it was all hands to the hay field. I used to help Mr Dinsdale turn hay by hand using a rake. Mrs Dinsdale and her daughter also gave a hand, the four of us going round the field turning the new cut swathe. Hay was strewed by hand rake, to help it dry better. When dry it was put into 'jockies' (hay cocks). Lemonade and beer were carried to the hay field, also a basket of food. Mr Dinsdale used a paddy sweep, pulled by one horse, brought the hay to the barn, then forked it through the forking hole; inside Mrs Dinsdale and I spread it about, trod it well down. Swallows used to keep coming into the barn to feed their young while outside the cuckoo was calling out.

Bracken growing on the fell side was cut, using a scythe, when dry it was loaded onto a sled and brought down to be put into a stack for bedding. When bedding the young stock up in the loose boxes, they had to be chased round the box to paddle it well in so that they did not eat too much bracken.

While I was still at school, Jim Wells asked if I would go with him each Saturday to help fill coal sacks and deliver them. Jim had a 30 cwt Ford truck which had to be started by a handle, even the windscreen wiper had to be worked by hand. Coal was weighed off at Wensley station, one hundredweight of coal cost 10d; best coal 1/1d a cwt. Times must have been very hard if a farmer was stocking up for winter. It was my job to see that an empty sack was put on the heap, so that the farmer only got 19 sacks, yet paid for 20, this was checked by counting the heap of empty sacks. Working from 7.30 a.m. until 6 p.m., I received 2/6d (12½ pence).

Mr Winsby, joiner and cabinet maker, Leyburn, wanted an apprentice.

I cycled to Leyburn to see him. He offered me 3/- (15 pence) a week to learn a seven year apprenticeship. Mother told me that for 3/-a week she would not be able to feed and clothe me, so I had better go to farm work where I would live in and get good food.

I was 14 years old on Friday 20th October 1937, and left school the same day, so did Nat who went to work in his father's butcher's shop, Ron Baddon and I to farm work. At school we were taught the 3 Rs, also 1 rod, pole or perch – 5½ yards, 4 poles – 1 chain (22 yards), 10 – chains – 1 furlong – 8 furlongs – 1 mile. All this came in useful when I left school and had to measure land out for turnips and potatoes in large fields. When the Ministry of Food representatives came round during the war they measured with a chain. One chain – one hundred links.

PLUMP HOUSE

Saturday morning, 21st October, with not a half penny in my pocket, I set off to cycle ten miles to Plump House, near Thornton Watlass, carrying a brown paper parcel in which was a change of clean underwear. I arrived in time for dinner, I knew Stanley and Mrs Trewhitt, also Tom Harker, the horseman, from when I lived at Finghall. Stan had taken over his father's farm in the May, I was his first lad. After dinner Stan loaned me a 410 single barrel shot gun. 'Here, tak this, we'll gan an walk the turnips ower, an don't dee owt daft wi it.' A gamekeeper called Chillman took Stan's rabbits to Bedale market each Tuesday, he had a motorbike and sidecar. Stan had borrowed the motorbike to come to East Witton to see mother about me going to work for him. I was to live in as one of the family, and receive 5/- (25 pence) a week wage. He fastened the bargain by giving mother a 2/- piece.

When the turnips and mangolds had been walked over I had three rabbits hanging from my waist. They had been legged, then some 'Billy band' put through, then tied round my waist. While walking over the fields, Stan was showing me his boundary fences, 'An think on which is ours, some farmers have got a hedge slashed for nowt with the hired man not knowing whose hedge it was.'

That night the cows were to turn out of the byre to drink at the pond by the roadside. They walked on their own, then back again, cars were few then. On foggy nights no lights were used to show that the cows were on the road. Stirks running loose in boxes were turned into a field to drink at the gutter, which soon turned into a puddle. The water in the gutter went into the pond, so the stirks had to be turned out last. 'Run round the hens and fasten them in, there's a lad.' After tea the cows were to milk, calves to feed, Mrs Trewhitt put the milk over the cooler.

'When I call you in the morning get up, I don't want to call you twice,' said Stan as I was going to bed. I had no watch and only my school clothes to work in. My bedroom was a small box room with a single bed against the wall, lino on the floor with a small prodded mat near the bed, a small round table for the candle to stand on, two nails behind the door on which to hang coats. The small window let you look across the road onto pasture land where in summer you could see the cattle grazing. The granary joined onto the house, and at night when in bed, I could hear rats squealing and scratching. Sometimes they seemed as if they would come through the ceiling.

When I was putting my boots on next morning, by the light of a stable lamp, the clock struck 5.30, milk pails were rattling, Stan came to see me with a lamp lit, 'Here, tak this, take care of it, deean't let me see it with a dirty glass, keep it full of paraffin, that's yours to look after.' I had to cool the milk, a 40 gallon tank of water stood on a wooden platform outside, near the kitchen wall. A rubber tube from the tank came through the wall, onto the bottom of the cooler. As the milk ran down, the water ran up inside the cooler, out through a tube into a pail, when nearly full the tube was taken out, put into another pail. I had to take the full one and empty the water back into the tank. The water was going round and round until all the milk had passed over the cooler, by this time the water was warm, it was then used for feeding the calves. The tank was then filled from a pump near the back door ready for the next cooling. Each morning five churns full of milk were put into the milk float, then taken to Jervo station at Newton-le-Willows, that was Tom Harker's job, the milk train came around 7.30 a.m.

Each night a slab of linseed cake and cotton cake had to be put through the cake crusher by hand, each slab was put in a separate bucket then boiling water poured over to fill up the bucket, this was for feeding the calves next morning. When cold it was a slimy mess. A pint measure had to used for the correct amount to be given to each calf, older ones having the most of the linseed and cotton mixture, with warm water added, the younger ones having milk, warm water and some of the slimy mixture added. 'Now think on which gets the most, I don't want them bloated,' said Stan.

I had not been at Trewhitt's very long when, sitting down to tea one night, there was a knock on the front door. It being dark, Stan went to the door and came back telling us, 'It's old William, mak him a sandwich and a mug of tea missus will you.' Old William was a tramp who over the years had slept in the stable overnight, when on his way to Leeds from Newcastle. Next morning he had breakfast, then a wash at the sink, drying himself on the 'hardin' towel, which we used to dry our hands on when washing them. He then split a few logs and went on his way again carrying a small bundle, shouting, 'I'll see you in the spring.'

It was near the end of November when Stanley said, 'I think we'll 'ev that fat pig killed, Billy Wilk will come and kill it for us, he always ez.' Saturday afternoon the copper was boiling, ready for Billy and his dad. They never walked together, always one behind the other shouting at one another as they walked along. We could hear them long before they came into sight.

The fat pig was brought out, screaming, on a length of plough cord, its feet were tied, then it was lifted onto the creel which stood near the back kitchen door on the cement. Old man Wilk stuck the pig to make it bleed, catching the blood in a bowl, he then asked me to, 'Stir that blood young man will ta, just put your hand in and give it a good stir up.' This I would not do. He went up the wall shouting at me, 'A young rascal like you never doing as he is told, you want your backside twilting for back-answering your elders.'

The pig was hung on a cawmbrill in the back kitchen for three days. That night after milking, Billy Wilk came to cut the pig up. My job then was crushing rock salt with a wooden roller ready for salting the sides of bacon and hams, salt petre and brown sugar were also used. Stan had a big trough specially for salting the sides and hams in, at one end there was a bung hole to drain the brine off to keep the bacon dry. When cured the bacon and hams were hung up in the living room where it was warm, then later in the gun room. Folks then were very superstitious, the wimmin folk had not to handle any of the bacon, as this would 'mak it gan rang', the moon had not to be on the wane, or a full moon when killing the pig.

At the beginning of December the thresher came in, it was 7 o'clock at night, for one day's threshing. How they managed to see with only a stable lamp dangling from the front axle, and a red one hung at the back swinging about, I never knew. 'Reet Dennis, bring your light, show him yon gate post, don't let him touch it, or it will be a gonner,' shouted Stan. The machine was set up alongside the oat stack ready for morning, the two men came in for supper, eating some of the pig cuttings.

'We'll be up in good tahm i't morning, an get a good start, thoo'll be cowling caff,' said Stan as I was going to bed.

I had seen a thresher at work but had never been allowed near one,

23

this was to be my first day threshing. After milking and all the stock had been fed, hens let out and fed, the two thresher men came in for breakfast with us. Coal and railway sacks had been brought from Jervo station, the men that came to help were from other farms, called borrowed men. Two kossiter sacks were opened up, then joined together with 'Billy band', these I had to use to carry the chaff in. At 8 o'clock the thresher started, dust and caff blowing about. Using the caff sheet I had to carry caff into all the loose boxes to bed them up, then carry it into a building for later use, wheat and oat chaff were only used for bedding. I was fed up by 'lowance' time, my boots were full of caff, my eyes full of dust, the caff kept bunging up, I could not move it fast enough. After the oats were done, the barley stack was next, then it was better for me, I had only to put the chaff into a heap. By night I was truly fed up, the day seemed never ending, all the men were new to me, I was shy and all alone. Really I did not know how they could laugh and joke while working so hard. My jumper was full of barley hawns, my hair, my socks full of prickly barley hawns, never been so tired before – then the machine stopped – tea and a rest? 'Before you come in for tea Dennis, just run round the hens and fasten them in, there's a lad.'

After tea the cows were to milk, calves to feed and the pigs, turnips to carry out, milk to cool. It was 8 o'clock when I stripped off to wash in the back kitchen. Mrs Trewhitt bringing me lots of hot water from the side boiler. We had sat down to supper when a loud knock came on the front door, then shouting. The steam engine with the thresher had pulled out of Stan's around 7 o'clock, going down the road to Mr Backhouse, who farmed at Thirn Moor, having told Stan they would fill up with water at Wash Beck. This is a stream which runs under the road. The engine had pulled onto the grass verge then sunk down, part of the engine resting on the road. 'Bring your lights and see what we can do.' Have you ever been tired? From the farm we walked half a mile to have a look, the engine was leaning over, bogged down, there were no telephones, it had to be left. 'Dennis, get up lad,' it was 5.30 a.m., start to another day.

> Ere the lark salute the skies,
> ere the sun upon us smile,
> From our warm beds we rise,

weary with the last day's toil.

All the barley chaff had to be led out of the stackyard with a horse and cart, into an old quarry for the pheasants to pick among. It was mid afternoon when an engine came to pull the other one out, we had time to go along and watch it being pulled out. The one that came had a wire rope on a big drum underneath, it pulled the thresher and engine out with ease.

The barley which had been threshed had to be put through a winnowing machine, which had to be turned by hand, this blew the dust off, took the small corn out, which was called hinder-ends. 20 quarters of barley were put up, or four tons. This had to be carried out of the granary onto the L.N.E.R. waggon which took it to Jervo station.

'Tak this gilt to the boar at Backhouse's, it's second on thee left down the road, thoo can't miss it,' said Stan. The young pig had a plough cord fastened to its back leg for me to hold it, I was given a stick to guide it with. It was then that I met Ken Backhouse.

'How-ay in an have a cup of tea with us.' That's how news from one farm to the other was passed on, but I had been told.

'Now when thoo gans don't tell 'em owt, keep it to yourself what goes on here, now think on, ave tell't th.'

'How's Stan getting on, how much did his heifer mak?'

'He didn't say.'

'Are your hens laying well?'

'Only midlin.'

'Are yer coos milking well?'

'We have too many dry bag ones.'

When I arrived back at the farm, Stan asked, 'Did they ask you in for lowence?'

'Yes.'

'Did ter tell 'em owt?'

'No.'

'Good, thoo's larnin.'

I had been at Stan's for five weeks when he asked me, 'Have you ever thout of gihan ti't pitchers?'

'No, I have no money, mother wants it to buy me some working clothes.'

It was then that I got a shilling a week extra. I cycled to Bedale for the first time that Saturday afternoon for a hair cut, which cost 4d. While at Bedale I saw some grey flannel trousers in Hector Mennell's shop, they were long ones and cost 5/11d (30 pence). I saved the shillings for six weeks, then went to buy the long trousers to wear on Sundays.

'This morning thoo mun give t' Missus a hand.' It was Monday morning, 'weshing day'. Water was to carry from a large tank which stood at the end of the Dutch barn, to fill the copper, logs and coal for the fire, clothes line to put out, the hens were to feed with warm crowdy (meal mixed with warm water), water to carry to fill the hen troughs.

Wherever Stan went on the farm, he took me with him. The few sheep were to look round, finding them all right, we then walked across the fields to the Boot & Shoe pub at Thirn. Brewster was the landlord, he took us into the kitchen where I sat down to have my first pint of shandy. Before leaving we had to have a look at his fat pig, Stan giving it much praise, the fatter the pig, the better it was.

Each Sunday I cycled the ten miles home to East Witton, for a bath and a change of clothing, giving mother the 5/- (25 pence). After dinner the tin bath was brought into the house in front of the fire for my bath, Mother making sure my neck and ears were clean and hair washed properly. One Sunday mother came in with some new corduroy breeches and hob-nailed boots. When I cycled back to the farm Stan gave me some leather leggings to complete my outfit, now I was able to do away with my school clothes.

Christmas came, there was no giving of presents, no excitement, only a few sprigs of holly put over the pictures and on top of the press. In the spring of 1938, Tom Harker the horseman informed us at the breakfast table that he was going to be married, that he would be leaving on May Day the 13th. 'I want a young man, yan that will get on with the job, not an old chap.' That was what Stan kept on telling me when working together. The *Darlington & Stockton Times* then had pages full of farm men wanted.

It was a sunny Tuesday afternoon in April, Stan was at Bedale market, my job, to get two loads of mangolds into the turnip house for the stock. The mangolds were in a pie behind the stackyard wall near the road. When I was busy filling the first load, an old man came walking along the road from Newton-le-Willows, he had travelled by train to Jervo station.

'I hear you want a 'ossman, young fellow?' said he.

I looked at him, he had no tie on, whiskers, and his mac over his shoulder.

'Yes we do, but not a tramp, the boss wants a young man to get on with the job,' said I.

'Dose he now?' he said and then went on his way.

When I went in for tea that night, he was sat at the table.

'Come in young man, the tramp 'as come to have tea with you.'

He was Stan's father.

Stan returned from Bedale market with news that barley was to come down in price – a drop of 2/- (10p) a quarter, or 6d (2½p) a cwt. down to 28/- (£1.40p) a quarter. This was a big blow when milk was to come down in price. A new man came in place of Tom Harker, he did not stay long. One afternoon when working the land for roots with the plough, the two horses came up to the road gate, dragging the plough over the grass field. Then came the man. He told Stan that the plough had caught a big stone knocking him out. Not long after that, at breakfast, the new man went all stiff. I was sitting next to him, so I gently lowered him to the floor.

'Just 'ez I bloody thowt, he's had a fit, I knew there were no big stones in yon field, he'll etta go,' growled Stan.

In his place came a daytal man from Newton-le-Willows, he only got paid for the hours that he worked. That summer I was hoeing turnips at night for 1½d a hundred yards, making myself 3d a night. In one week I made 1/3d. When haytime came, all the hay was to strew round the hedge backs by hand, a paddy sweep was used for saming up the hay to make pikes. To save money, the daytal man went home at 5 o'clock. After tea I had to clean rake the fields using the horse and rake and lead pikes in under the Dutch barn, using a pike bogey. Five pikes had to be brought in ready for forking up the next morning. Rent day was coming, so Stan took a new calved cow to sell at Leyburn market. A good cow sold for £28. Things were getting bad, lambs were not worth taking to market, some making as little as 6/- each, rabbits which ran about in thousands, had no sale.

In October 1938, I had a 4/- (20p) pay rise for being a 'grand larl worker'; my week's pay was now 10/- (50p). I had to snag turnips when it was cold with early morning frost on them. Having no gloves on, my hands were blue with cold so Stan gave me some old socks to put on them. There was no rest for me on a Saturday afternoon, it was carrying sacks of oats for grinding, or helping when sawing logs, I had to use the wheelbarrow and take them into the stick house near the back door.

Saturday afternoon once a month I had to clean the four hen huts out. 'Tak't 'oss an t'cart, fower bags of caff, yan for each house, mak a good job of 'em, and think on, pull 'em on ti fresh grund, an put fresh watter in ti each trough.'

Another Christmas came, it was now 1939, the winter of 1938-9 had heavy snowfalls. The milk no longer went to the station, Northern Dairies had a wagon coming round picking the milk up at the farms, which made it much better. Now I was able to chop turnips, crush slabs of cow cake like other men, good food had built me up. I was able to put hay and straw mixed through a hand chopper for the horses with ease.

Things were bad for everyone, not only workers, even the news on the wireless was talk of war. Manure had to be led out from the midden onto the stubble field which was for mangolds and turnips, it was all spread by hand. A young man came to help with the harvest that year, I think he was trying to get into agriculture, then, if a war started he would be safe from call up. When we had finished stooking the first field of oats there was an odd shaff. Stan told the young man that a binder never threw an odd shaff out, he must have left one in the hedge back. Off he went to look for it.

'Let the silly bugger go, if he ez no more sense, he's not worth keeping,' said Stan. After all the stooks had been led in, hen huts with cock chickens in were taken onto the stubble fields, this was called stubbling, the chickens cleaned up all the loose corn. I had to watch over them each night to see that they did not stray too far from the huts, water and crowdy had to be carried each day.

The harvest of 1939 was very good weather. On Sunday, September 3rd I was cycling home to East Witton when a car stopped and the driver asked if I would like to hear the declaration of war on his car radio, this was the first radio I had seen in a car.

That October I was snagging turnips when the fox hounds came onto the farm. That afternoon a man on a hunter came to where I was snagging, I had seen him before, he was a farmer called Spink.

'Your boss tells ma he ez ti pay thee 17/- (85 pence) a week to keep thee here. I'll give you a pund a week if thoo will come ti work for me.'

'You will!'

'Yes ah wad, if ter comes thoo'll be second 'ossman tiv our Joe. Thoo can be at my place by Martinmas, and thoo waint ev all them coos to see ti,' said he.

When I told Stan that I had chance of more money he told me that he could not afford to pay any more.

ROOKWITH GRANGE

On Saturday, November 11th, after having dinner I left Plump House. Stan and I had parted good friends, he gave me the tin trunk which he had loaned me to keep my clothes in at the farm. With the trunk on the bicycle I set off to walk over the fields to Rookwith Grange, after two years at Plump House, and not one day off.

Rookwith Grange stands in the middle of fields, half a mile inland from any road, on the Jervaulx Estate. The main entrance to the farm is at Rookwith. This lane is used by motor vehicles to the farm. There is a cart track over the fields to Thirn, not very good in wet weather when walking; a better cart track through Stan's fields leads to the Newton-le-Willows road.

Looking round the farm buildings before tea, I was shown a yellow

Rookwith

Ford tractor on spade lugs which started on petrol then ran on T.V.O. (tractor vaporising oil). 200 gallons then cost £11.0.0. There was a Morris car which had a fold up rack on the back, which was used to carry boxes of eggs to market, or transport the 12 gallon churn of milk onto the stand at Rookwith in summer, when the horses were out to grass on a Sunday morning. The milk was picked up by Rowntree of Masham. The large foldyard was full of fat beasts, with pigs running amongst them. There was also a stable with four working horses and two hunters for following the hounds. Each house had its own atmosphere. I knew when I sat down to tea that this was a friendly one, six sat down for meals each day. Sunday morning, I had my first lay in bed from leaving school. 7 o'clock instead of 5.30 a.m. Breakfast was at 9 o'clock, this was to give the 'wimmin' folk a rest.

The farm was cut in two by the Thirn to Rookwith road; the land over the road was called Mooser, here there were 30 young beasts in a large foldyard. After breakfast three of us walked the half mile to water them, rack them well up with hay and lots of chopped turnips to last the day. This would save walking back at night.

'Yer'll be gihan ti choch wi our Joe ti neet, I like to see young folk gihan ti choch.' So we walked to church each Sunday night at Thornton Watlass.

My bed was in the same large room as Joe and Mick, I had no use of a wardrobe and drawers. When in bed at night there were no rats scratching and squealing, the farm house was separate from the farm buildings. Out of the bedroom window, Witton Fell could be seen in the distance. Mrs Spink was not very well, Miss Hunter was the housekeeper, Joyce Hunt the maid, Joe the eldest son, and George, the second son who was always called Mick. The 'Gaffer' as he liked to be called, walked with a limp, having been kicked off a horse when he was younger. On his face was the mark of a horse shoe where it had cut into the flesh, the gaffer spoke in dialect, a true Yorkshire man, a TYKE.

'WHAT IS A TYKE'?

A Yorkshire man who must be very carefully watched, especially at horse and cattle sales, the most accomplished 'whisperers, fakers and lifters'. We are painted as shrewd, to be able to hold our own with all comers, yet simple, half-witted, clod-hopping fools, wearing a smock and bordering on imbecility. A yokel of very low mentality, slow of speech, slow of thought, awkward of gait, a harmless, clownish, hobble-de-hoy, an easy prey when one is in search of a simpleton. A red-nosed, open-mouthed idiot, when portrayed on stage or screen, an inarticulate lunatic in a smock. To be silent as dumb-driven cattle, too reticent to open our mouths, possessed of such slow-working brains that we cannot marshal our thoughts and words into coherent, articulate expression. Yet all blow their own trumpet in the North Countree.

J. Fairfax – Blakeborough.

The blackout in the farm buildings was not up to standard, lime wash with sheep dip added to make it darker, was brushed onto all glass window lights from inside the buildings, then a thick cotton cake sack nailed over each window light.

Doors which opened into the foldyard had curtains made from Kossiter sacks hung down them. (Kossiter was flake maize made from Indian corn, better known today as Corn Flakes.) It was fed to all stock, the two farm dogs ate it with warm milk on. The curtains made it much easier to carry the skeps of turnips through when feeding the stock, not having to close the door each time. When dark, any light showing through the roof of the buildings had to be plugged with straw, that was my job up in the rafters. Even finger holes in the doors had a wisp of hay pushed in at night, the blackout was secure, when there was no moon not a light could be seen.

All stable lamps were to be put out before leaving the buildings and walking to the farm house, which was separate from the buildings. The geese were put into two lots, one on the North side of the farm house where the pond was, others in the garth at the South side. The two farm dogs were free to run about at night, then if any one came during the night the dogs or geese would give us warning.

Each morning when the gaffer called for us to arise, which was before six o'clock, he always had something to tell us, such as;

'Come men, get up, there's Broadwith's men been up an hour, an you lot still liggin i' bed.'

Christmas, there was frummety with rum added, rum sauce on Christmas pudding, wine with cake and cheese. How well I remember the gaffer sharpening the knife to carve the goose, then looking round the table saying, 'I suppose you all want a leg, a wing, and a bit off the breast, I'll see what I can do, I'll have a six-legged goose next year.'

Spring came, the news on the wireless about the war was not very good. Living in the country, the war seemed far away, everything was peaceful. It was lovely to hear the birds in the morning, the fields around had plovers and skylarks in abundance, a train whistle could be heard from far away.

At the beginning of May a young man started to work for Spink, Gill Moss, who came from Thornton Watlass. Gill took me to his home and to meet other young lads in the village. Now I had someone to go about with when cycling to the pictures at Bedale and the village dances.

One hour extra had been put on the clocks for summer time, making it two hours in front of the sun. Probably it helped those in the towns but it was no use for the farmers. It was while I was luking corn, a monotonous job following the drill bredes all day, stubbing thistles out with a 'jobber', lifting docks out, carrying them in a sack which was carried over the shoulder, then spreading them on the cart track for the cart wheels to crush, that the gaffer came with news of Dunkirk. 'Things leeak bad, men. Hitler will seean be here.'

May 14th, Anthony Eden broadcast over the wireless for 'Local Defence Volunteers.' Dunkirk was the last stand for the British Army. Richard Spink was sure the Germans would come marching up to his farm.

The following day the four of us went to volunteer at Thornton Watlass, taking the three farm shot guns with us. Really we did not know quite what to do or what to expect. Mr Tucker, a farmer who had served in the First World War, took charge. Mr Moss, Gill's father who had also served in the war, gave advice on what to do. Work on all the farms came to a standstill. Nights were the biggest problem, that was when parachutists in small numbers were expected to be dropped. Invasion was a real possibility. There being no telephone, Arthur Simpson the postman, came round on his bicycle to let us know when there was an invasion scare on. Messages came from the Bedale police. Shot guns were taken into the fields when working. I had the loan of a shot gun from Mr Tucker, the 50 cartridges had steel balls inside, more powerful than those with pellets in.

How-ay men, get up, think of your country, there's a war on, or doesn't it bother you, just for once show willing.

I was the only one who did not smoke among the men at the farm. Woodbines then were 4d for a packet of ten. Because I did not smoke I had to be the first one into the buildings each morning, as I would have a better chance of smelling cigarette smoke if anyone had been in the buildings during the night. We got a start carrying the shot guns with us each morning when going to milk. Many a time the cows were never milked at night, the one stood near the byre door would be let in and milked for the house. Sometimes all the milk would be fed to the pigs, each morning I had a pint of warm milk to drink which had only been put through the sile.

Invasion was a real possibility. In July 1940, when the L.D.V. became the Home Guard, soldiers from Catterick Camp came to instruct us on weapons. More Spitfires were flying about, sometimes two days in succession. We were in the fields around Thornton Watlass, watching the skies for enemy aircraft dropping parachutists. My thanks to the good folk of Thornton Watlass for supplying tea and sandwiches after spending a nervous day out in the fields. Mr Moss came to tell us which house to call at for tea and they were remembered when pig killing came round.

Sunday work, which had never been done before, had to be done to catch up with the backlog of work, through us having time off for Home Guard duties. During the night, one year after the war had started, bombs were dropped over our fields. One bomb fell in a smallholder's field belonging to Mr Musgrave, killing one of his cows. Eight bombs were dropped, also incendiary bombs. What a rumble in the early morning! There was no going back to bed, stock in the fields had to be looked at. The bomb craters had to be inspected by the army before we were able to fill them in, they took shrapnel away with them.

Soldiers in trucks and light tanks were always on the Rookwith to Thirn road. It did not take them long to find out that milk was in the churn waiting to be collected. Many a time Spink had half a churn missing, (5 gallons) but he never complained.

'They might ez well have it ez Hitler.' Milk then would be 9d a gallon.

Get up men, or do you want the day off to lig in bed, if you do just say and you can eft, so long as you get up to milk fost.'

Midsummer, 5 o'clock in the morning, after working until the sun went down, with two hours on the clock, it was nearly midnight when the day's work was done.

At breakfast that morning the gaffer said, 'In the morning Dennis, you will etta be up in good tahm, ti gan an cut grass for Frank Maidment. Croft wants his cutting ez well, that will keep thee gihan ivvery morning this week.'

As dawn was breaking, two horses were geared up then yoked into the grass cutter. Four acres of grass were cut while it was cool before the flies and clegs annoyed the horses; after breakfast the potatoes were to furr up for the last time; in the afternoon hay had to be sammed up with a paddy sweep to make pikes; this went on until sundown, to make up for lost time at the Home Guard.

In 1941, a second lot of bombs fell on Mooser land near the River Ure. One bomb which fell in Sam Harker's field, failed to explode, a mine on a parachute had a direct hit on the White Bear Hotel, Masham, killing those inside. Sam Harker who farmed at Hellming found the unexploded bomb, he had walked up to the mound of earth. He then informed East Witton Home Guard and Sam Harker with Ralph Maughan, went on horseback to inspect the bomb. While they were tying their horses to the gate to walk to the bomb, it exploded. They were very lucky, old Sam was unable to speak for two days, being in shock.

The Pioneer Corps were billeted in part of Clifton Castle, they unloaded the truck loads of ammunition that came along the roadsides. We were hoeing turnips when the gaffer came to tell us that a beast at Mooser was bleeding from the mouth so we had to drive some of them to Grange Farm. On inspection, we found that one side of the beast's tongue was missing, it had been caught in a snare. The soldiers at Clifton had been trying to catch a few rabbits by setting snares. The beast had to be fed on gruel for days, something we could have done without.

Words which fall from the old folks' lips, may sound uncouth to the ear untaught.

'You lot deean't know how lucky you are, gahin ti't pitchers an dancing yance a fot'neet. When I was your age I could nivver gan tiv a dance or owt like that, I had ti gan an work to arn a living.

'I allus thowt of t'boss, ti do him a bit of good, you lot cudn't care less about the farm. It wadn't bother you lot if Hitler cam ti tak it ower. Ah saw thee Dennis, talking tiv Broadwith's maid t'other day, thoo wants nowt wi her, she'll nobbut squander thee brass. Stanley ez a maid far better than you. Our Joe owt ti get 'issen wed, an thoo, our George, give ower gihan ti Croft's sa mich, thoo's gihan ti spend all before you, what wi that an smoking. Ah's gihan ti be begged.

'We could dee wi some mair sheep netting, but Ah doubt whether it wad get put up. When I was your age I could carry thur'teen stakes, mell, crow bar and a net, you lot want a 'oss and cart for ivvery thing. Ya thing Ah notice, yer not slow at eating, you all like yer grub. Yer not slow when it comes ti running off ti't Home Guard, that's because you are running away from work. The only good workers I know on this farm are Miss Hunter and Joyce here. It taks them all day and ivvery day ti fettle grub for you lot. Now if you teeak a leaf out of their book, you wad get mair work deean outside.

'Broadwith tells ma his men are allus keen ti start work, he ez a job ti hod 'em back frev it. You lot stand and leeak at it ower lang, that's your trubble.

'I suppose you all want some holidus, thoo'll ef ti ev some, ev a day or tweea off Dennis, when we ain't mich on, or when it's wet, that's if you can fin'd anywhere ti gan, it's nay use gihan ti Redcar, it's all fenced off wi barbed wire an land mines. Ah'll bet it didn't tak them soldiers lang ti put it up, you lot wad tak twice ez lang.

'After breckus men, we'll a'e ti ev some draft yows drawn out, an ta'en ti Bedale mart, an ev a bit of a sale ti keep the job going. You all want paying, even if there's nowt to show for it. Coo pasture is all winn'l straes, there's nowt fo't beast ti eat wi all this plooin out. But then we must leeak efter't soldiers, keep them well fed, they do a good job an tak less pay than you blokes.

'After breeakus, thoo mun get a start ti ploo, our Joe will keep thee right, he'll show yer how ti mark a field out correctly, throw the rigg oppen and close it in.' So said the gaffer.

You can't mak brass wi liggin i'bid, if I were you lot, ar'd get up an mak some, that's if you ev owt about yer.'

From the living room of the farm house, a door opened onto some stairs which led up to a large back room, the floor was covered with hand-picked apples. In this large room stood a bath, there was no running water to it. Water was heated in the copper each Friday night, then in turn you carried your own water up the stairs, and when done, emptied the bath ready for the next one. This saved me getting bathed at home.

When possible, the gaffer liked us all to be in the house by ten o'clock at night and believe me, you were pleased to go to bed. Our days were long, trying to keep up with the seasonal work, not knowing when you may be called out early morning for Home Guard duties. Many a time we have been going in for supper at midnight, then up next morning before six o'clock. Some days we were on the go for eighteen hours, resting only at meal times.

Each time the men from the Ministry of Agriculture came round the farm, there was more land to plough out, more potatoes to plant. The Government told the farmers what to grow, that way they knew how much barley, wheat etc, was in the country, also what stock was on the farm.

Winter months when all stock was laid in, each night before supper they were to look round, to see that all was well and comfortable, the horses were given more clover hay, their bedding shaken up. The two farm dogs used to follow us around to chase the rats, especially in the barn where the cow cake was kept. One night when going round, we came across a calf laid on its back in the feeding trough; while struggling to get out, it had smashed the back of its head in, it died while we were lifting it out. The older beast had bumped it into the trough, next morning the muck had to be led out and the trough lifted up.

The farm water came from a spring at Sand Hill. It was never known to run dry. There was a tap in the back kitchen over the sink, one outside which filled the horse trough, where the milk churn stood when cooling the milk. When the water was running slow, we had to take the cinders out of the filter bed and give them a good wash before putting them back. The overflow from the spring went into a trough to water Sand Hill stock.

Mr Tucker was made Lieutenant in command of Thornton Watlass Platoon, Mr Moss made sergeant. How well I remember the first church parade the Home Guard had. Marching from the village to the church, carrying our rifles which were left in the vestry with Arthur Simpson standing guard over them. Harry Carlin and Harry Kitchen on the look out for parachutists, stood on the church tower. If any had been seen, the church bells would have been rung. No stranger would travel very far in the country, they were all eyed with suspicion, there was usually someone who would know others from the villages around, as I did.

What a buzz of excitement there was one Thursday night when Mr Tucker told us that on the Sunday coming, the Home Guard were going onto the rifle ranges on Bellerby Moor. Two army trucks came at eight o'clock that Sunday morning. We all had our boots, buttons, and rifles polished, looking our best, even if some uniforms were on the big side. Shoulder flashes showed HOME GUARD in a yellow crescent, in a square below, 11th N.R.BATT. We were taken to Deer Bolt Rifle Range which I expected to be deserted in such an isolated place. Soldiers from the Green Howards were there to keep us right, truck loads of Home Guard came from the villages around the Bedale area, mostly farm men and gamekeepers. We had to pass in orderly line through a brick-built building, where seated behind a long bench, soldiers took our name and rifle number. We were then given 15 rounds of 303 ammunition each and told to bring back the empty shells. Hundreds took part that first day on the ranges.

'Right, follow me!' shouted the Sergeant, who had lined us up. 'Left, right.' The Home Guard came under the same rules as the army when in uniform.

'This is the target area.' Twenty targets stood behind a huge hill, black circles on a white background. 'The bull is where you aim for,' said the sergeant. 'Then you have inners, outers and magpies, have you got that?' We were shown a white disc on a long pole for marking.

'If the bullet hole is to the left, the marker has to be swung to the left and placed over the hole, same for the right, have you got that? If top or bottom, the marker goes up and down, for a magpie, the marker is twisted round and round. Have you got that?'

Behind where the markers stood, a building had been built into the hill, this was where the targets were taken when putting new ones on. The targets moved up and down in a frame pulled by a rope on pulleys.

The sergeant in charge marched us back. 'You are now 600 yards from the target, you lie prone on the grass here, fire 5 rounds, run 200 yards to that hill you see in front, 5 rounds rapid fire, then you run into the trench which is 200 yards from the target and fire at will, have you got that? Each firing line will have a soldier manning a telephone which is in contact with the markers. When he gives the command, commence firing, if a red flag comes up, STOP immediately. Have you got that?'

Had we done our drill right in the fields back home? Aim, squeeze, hold your breath – Crack – the first shot had gone, it was far better than a 12 bore shot gun. Word went up the line, 'There's nowt to it.'

Behind stood the Army Officers with binoculars, watching. It was three o'clock when rifles were being cleaned, after handing in our empty shells. We were lined up at the pick-up point when an Army Officer stood in front of us and said, 'A bloody good show, we have men who come here and miss the bloody target, good luck.'

The army trucks took us to Catterick Camp, where we had a mug of tea with a doorstep sandwich of bully beef. Each man was allowed to buy a 2d bar of chocolate at the canteen (sweets were on ration). We arrived at Thornton Watlass by 5 o'clock, Mr Tucker was very proud of his platoon.

Four hours on Tuesday and Thursday nights and all day Sunday, 8 a.m. to 5 p.m, were given up for the Home Guard. Some nights were spent out in the fields around Watlass going from A to B without being seen.

One half of the platoon had to watch for the other half going into a wood, or from field to field, that way we found out the best cover. To help, extra rails were put onto some gates, old implements put into hedge gaps, sheep racks were used in the fields to get near sink holes, these were filled with stones, the wheels then let into the ground, so that the stock when rubbing on them did not move them. In some cases, sacks were nailed onto the bottom of gates, so that we were able to crawl past on our stomach without being seen. Holes were made in hedges to crawl through where it was thick. When soldiers were hiding in sink holes, acting as parachutists, animals in the fields gave them away, they would stand and look at them.

It was in the winter months that the army was attacking Bedale, as usual they were the parachutists. Newton-le-Willows sent a message that some parachutists were walking down the railway line. The Home Guard chose its place for an ambush to surprise them, a dozen soldiers came walking past, our chinese crackers were fired to let them know they had been fired on. Did they stop! Not they. With shouts of, 'Bloody afternoon soldiers, we are just playing silly buggers for the sake of you lot, it's you who were shot not us!' they kept on walking down the line towards Bedale. This caused a lot of arguments with the men in white coats (umpires).

A Lewis machine-gun had been allocated to Watlass platoon, Dick Gatenby being Number 1 gunner. I was chosen as Number 2. Hand grenades were issued, two to a man; each man carried a 303 rifle with one hundred rounds of ammunition, a bayonet, steel helmet, gas mask and cape, also some very hard biscuits called emergency rations.

I have seen a bill made out in 1892:

		Translation:	
oss af a da	1/6d	Horse half a day	1/6
a fot oss	1/6d	Hay for horse	1/6
takinonimbakagan . .	1/6d	Taking him back again . . . 1/6	
	4/6d		

That bill was made out long before I was born but when I think back it was not much better when I started work in 1937. The bills sent out by

Mr Leyburn, blacksmith, Newton-le-Willows, were not much better, but we could still understand them. 'Shooin oss', was quite common on the bills that I paid for R. Spink in the 40s. We wrote as we spoke, it was understandable to us.

'Thoo'd better gan for a leead of coal this morning, tak Nance wi yer, an git 'em beeath shod, deean't git mair than a ton, use yan ez a trace oss.'

When I arrived at the blacksmith's there was a new owner, Bert Langdon, who had been Mr Leyburn's apprentice, he had taken over to work for himself. When at the blacksmith's you never stood to watch, there was the fire to blow up, something to hold, water to carry for the trough for cooling the red hot iron. After the first horse had been shod it was yoked into the cart. Then to the station for the coal, where the horse and cart were weighed, I stood in front of the horse to hold it still on the moving platform. When weighing the load of coal, I stood as before but on the firm ground, having my weight extra in coal. When I called at the blacksmith's for the second horse, it was used as the trace horse. The three miles to the farm were soon covered, the horses going faster back home.

Chip barrows, seed barrows, all were taken to the blacksmith, parts off ploughs, grubbers off scrufflers, wheels off carts for rehooping, cow chains, axles off sheep racks, hinges for the lids, which were always being broken with the horses and cows rubbing on them. As more and more grass land came under the plough, this brought the cows, sheep and horses together, fences were being broken down. The boundary fence had to be walked regularly. I loved doing woodwork, in my spare time I mended hen huts, sheep racks and doors. There was nowhere to go, no signposts to let anyone know which way to go, not even the village name at the Post Office or shop.

There had been an invasion scare on and through the day the Home Guard had been in the fields around Watlass, keeping out of sight under the hedges in the dry ditches and hollows, on the look out for parachutists. The two roads, the Bedale to Masham road by Snape road end, the Bedale Burrill road were under surveillance all day. Little did those farmers know they were being watched while looking round their stock.

A hollow had been dug in the village green for the machine-gun to be set up, sand bags were around the perimeter, every vehicle passing through the village had to be stopped and identity cards shown. Frank Maidment, who had been with us all day, farmed at Thirn. He told us that he was going home to milk, then to Bedale to meet someone off the bus. Later he came into the village with his car, wearing civilian clothes. He was stopped, asked to show his I.D. card which he did not carry, he was escorted into the vicarage with fixed bayonets.

'You know me, you daft buggers, I want to meet a bus in Bedale in ten minutes.'

'How do we know who you are without your identity card? You could be helping the Germans?'

He was held in the vicarage where the Home Guard had their Head Quarters, for a joke, also to teach him to carry an I.D. card.

One call out I well remember: the Home Guard from Masham to Bedale and Hackforth were called out, bringing in Snape, Newton-le-Willows and Crakehall. Snape and Thornton Watlass had over one hundred men in the Home Guard. At 5 o'clock in the morning the Home Guard was ready to search every wood, hollows in the fields which had to be approached very carefully, stone barns and hen huts were all to be checked out. Walking from east to west, until we came in contact with the Home Guard coming from the west, then the search would end. When the four of us arrived back at the farm around 11 o'clock the gaffer asked, 'Hi-ya shot out, men?'

The Home Guard had got into a routine, trees had been marked for felling across the roads, especially where there were deep cams such as Hell Hole and the Fox Covert roads. This would have given us the chance to lob hand grenades onto German trucks or light tanks. Holes were made in walls, especially those alongside the roadside, just large enough to see through and shoot.

The Home Guard had been issued with high explosive in a rectangular container, which was about 2 inches thick and 5 inches long, by 4 inches wide. A thin wire was fastened to it, which allowed you to pull it from one side of the road to the other. They would have been used where the holes in the walls had been made, to enable it to be pulled under the tracks of tanks or other vehicles to disable them.

By working faithfully eight hours a day, you may eventually get to be the boss and work twelve hours a day.

'Thoo's eighteen now, an old eneeaf ti hug corn Dennis, thoo'll be with Joe and Jim Gatenby, we'll start on't oats fost ti get thee brokken in.'

Oats were carried in any given weight, barley in 16 stone railway sacks. It was May, the last two days threshing, coals and sacks had been brought from Jervo station.

'When thoo gans ti't Home Guard ti neet, call on Rab, tell him we'er gihan ti thresh.'

Rab lived in a cottage between Thirn and Watlass, 'How-ay in Den, an sit thee sen down.' When I went in, Rab and his wife Mable had a sack of tails docked from foals in front of a blazing fire, they were busy cutting the hair off them. Mable was the band cutter when the thresher came into the district. When I carried corn I had 2/6d (12½p) a day extra. I did very well when the thresher came, going to other farms as a borrowed man. All stacks were made out in the fields, wire netting was put round the stacks when threshing to help catch the rats. When Joe and I went to other farms we always took a look at their stock and fat pig. When sat down to dinner each farmer had his own tale to tell. Mr Hudson of Marriforth, a chapel man known as the 'Bounder' because he did not swear, told this tale.

'Our sheep had got out into the next door neighbour's field, in among their sheep, larl bitch was straining on her chain to go after them. So I let her loose, away she went, sorted ours out from theirs, brought ours back through the gap into our field, counted them, found one missing, then went back for it. After she had brought it back, she went and found a whin bush, pulled it up, then pulled it into the gap. You can believe me or believe me not!'

Backhouse, Thirn Moor Farm, good homely folk, always made you welcome, very good food, they told this tale.

'We'd been missing coal. Ah thowt someone wer getting it, an this neet Ah 'eeard t'dog barking, making sik a noise that Ah let him lowse. Ah could see him mak his way up t' field, then Ah spotted a man gihan away wi a sec of coal on his back, an duster know ez he jump t' off t' rails on ti't road, that dog of mine let go at him, an dizta know that dog of mine bit t' top rail clean i' two.'

Give a difficult task to a lazy man, and he'll find an easier way of doing it.

'After breeakus, thoo mun get a start to plough, our Joe will keep you right.' Braffen, yams, blinders, backband with trace chains were to put on the two horses. I had ploughed before and knew all the parts which made up the plough. The main beam, stilts, mould-board, landside, coulter, wing and sock. When yoking horses to the plough, a rocktree, swingletree, crabtree, were used. A few bits of bottry (common elderberry) were used as rigg sticks, all riggs had to be thrown open, then closed in, that way all the land was ploughed. Some good advice from Joe, 'If the old man brings your lowance, and wants you to drop the land wheel one sixteenth, just tak your plough key and tap it, that will please him.'

A searchlight had been set up in a field belonging to Mr Tucker. The men who came with it were Southerners. When they came into the Boot and Shoe pub at Thirn, we found their accents so different to ours, making it hard for us to understand them. With so much extra grass land having to be ploughed out, the talk in the pub then was the best way to plough the short furrs in a field when using a tractor with a trailer plough. The Southerners looked on in amazement, when tables and chairs were put to one side to clear the floor, then pint and gill glasses spaced out to represent the riggs, each man demonstrating how he would plough the short furrows.

Winter nights while playing cards, we all discussed what to do the next day, or when to do it, each one had his say. One later October night while playing cards, Joe brought the subject up of loading mangolds with a gripe, instead of throwing them in by hand after snagging them. That same day we had seen Broadwith's men loading mangolds with a gripe. Without a doubt, it was the one subject which was most discussed, the gaffer had the whole pie going rotten, from then on we never filled the carts by hand. The gaffer gave in with these words, 'Ah think ower much about yer, that's my problem, that's why I let you lig in bed so long ev a morning.'

Spring time at Rookwith Grange was really lovely, after all the dark, damp days of December, the snow and frosts of January, then the rain and mud of February, into March with its strong winds. As they lengthen, the warm days feel like spring, it was then that the plovers came back onto the ploughed land. It was good to hear them call out, curlew and snipe came onto the pasture land at Sand Hill Farm and High Rookwith, with Grange Farm being well inland there was a lot of bird life all round. When ploughing for roots, sea gulls came screaming near to the plough, when the furrow turns over they got trapped by their legs. I had to stop the plough to release them, this happened many times through the day.

As the warm spring sun penetrated the hedge backs it brought out the wild flowers which were in abundance, everything was lovely and fresh with the trees breaking into full leaf, young, fresh grass showing in the cow pasture. Each day the larks rose higher, sang longer, the gulls no longer came to follow the plough or harrows, rooks and other small birds had taken their place. Wagtails were in abundance when drilling corn with horses. Some days only the sound of the birds broke the silence, other days, guns being fired on the Bellerby moors rumbled on all morning, the drone of engines from the fighter planes added to the noise, then all was quiet again.

Young lambs were born in the paddock which had been wired round with sheep netting to help keep the foxes out. Also in the paddock were coops with young goslings in, and clockers with chickens. When the goslings were old enough they were allowed onto the pond where moor hens nested, their numbers never seemed to increase; magpies were hunting around the pond, maybe they found their eggs. May and June, the cornfields were a lovely green, all the trees in full leaf, the cuckoo calling out each day as we hoed turnips and mangolds. Woodpeckers were busy hammering at the trees in the wood nearby, young rabbits ran about in thousands, stoats and weasels were in every hedge, when all was quiet, you could hear a rabbit squeal out, we knew that a stoat or a weasel had got one.

Letter Box field, so called because a tree which stood in the hedge on the cart-road side had a hole in it where the postman left the *Yorkshire Post* paper and unimportant letters to be picked up. When ploughed out it had a good crop of wheat on, two big stacks had been made near the cart-road side. All stacks were made out in the fields, the Government had advised this on account of what they called the '5th column' going round setting fire to farm sheds full of corn. The weather had been fine and dry with hard frosts, a load of coal and 200 railway sacks had been brought from Jervo station, a tank on the flat rulley filled with water, all ready for the last week in November to thresh the two stacks. All the borrowed men had arrived, the thatch was being taken off when it started to snow. 'Give ower men, an we'll see what it is gahin ti dee,' said the gaffer. The steam engine was taken from the stacks, snow piled up, deep snow came, then frost. The owner of the engine came each day to light the fire in the engine to stop the boiler from freezing up. It was six weeks before the two stacks were threshed.

'By God men, Palmer the station master wants five weeks demurrage on yon 200 seks, it will cost the 'orth. I'll gan an see him, it's surprising what a few eggs and a piece of bacon can dee.'

(200 sacks at 1d each times five weeks – 1000d or £4-3-4d). Food being rationed, Mr Palmer took the eggs and bacon.

When threshing, hinder-ends were saved for such times as deep snow, they were taken into Ostler Brass wood for the pheasants and other birds to pick among. One year when harvest had finished, Joe and I were busy thatching the last corn stack, when it came a severe gale with rain lasting all night and day. It began to blow the end out of the wheat stack that we had been thatching. All that we were able to do in such conditions was to rope the chip-harrows onto the end of the stack. While we were doing this, the gaffer came riding up on his hunter, he had been looking round the stock at Mooser, and came to let us know that the River Ure was rising fast. 'Get your guns men, an gan an shut some rabbits.' We arrived just in time, the flood water was bringing the rabbits out, sheep and rabbits were floating down the river. The rabbits we shot were left for the flood water to take away. Later we found out that a farmer at Jervaulx, Mr Broadly, had lost up to thirty sheep in the flood.

Things are that bad men, all I ev put by for a rainy day is a pair of dry beeats, an you lot cudn't care less.

'Yon oats want oppening out this morning, and don't forget, you want a 11 foot swing for a 7 foot cut, then the binder can get round nicely.'

All corn fields had to be mown round with a lea (scythe), this made it so that no corn was trampled down when the binder pulled by three horses opened it out ready for the Fordson tractor to pull it. Joe and I did the scythe work, while Mick and Gill made the sheaves (pronounced shaves), using a gathering rake, and making bands out of the straw, which was a back-breaking job. The sheaves when made were stood up in the hedge-back, sparrows in large flocks came to feed off them. Cushats (pigeons) played havoc on the laid patches. The pros and cons of opening the fields out with the binder were discussed at tea that night. There must be a faster and cheaper way of opening a field out. The gaffer was on about the waste of corn, it was finally agreed that only each corner would be opened out to save time.

It was late September, a lovely harvest afternoon when cutting wheat, that the main cog on the binder broke. Mick went to Gill's of Leeming Bar but they did not have one. I had to accompany Mick to Wath near Ripon, to Bushells, the McCormick dealer, the petrol ration had to suffer, arriving back at the farm in time for tea. After tea that late September night, the binder out in the field was covered over with a stack sheet, sheaves were placed around the bottom of the sheet to keep the light in. With only a stable lamp to see with, Joe and I set to to replace the broken cog, which took until midnight; there was no moon, it was very still, at the slightest rumble the cock pheasants shouted out.

Get stooked up and have the rest of the day off.

That year, November 2nd, 1942, I had to have a medical for the Army at Darlington. I had to 'present myself before the Board of Examiners at 10 o'clock'. This was my first full day off work from leaving school. On the afternoon of the 1st November I cycled to East Whitton, then by bus to Leyburn, where I had to wait for the United bus coming from Hawes to Darlington, where I was able to stay the night at my Aunt Edna's in Cockerton village. The next morning I was able to go by tram into Darlington. I passed A1 at the medical, my call up for the Forces being put off for six weeks, being a farm worker was more important than being in the Army. After six weeks I received another letter, 'Your call up has been deferred for six weeks.' This went on until the landing in France for the second front.

When I was your age, my boots were nivver cold, I could nivver lig i'bed sa lang ez you lot, I wadn't want to anyway.'

Jim Jackson had left a steam engine at the side of the lane leading to Rookwith, I always passed it each morning taking the milk onto the stand. It had stood there for over two months. When I was passing one morning just before harvest started, I heard someone shouting from the engine, 'Help me, help me!' On investigating I found a man fast inside the fire-box. He was Freddy Brown from Patrick Brompton, a little thin man with cross eyes, but very good with steam engines. He had got inside to give it a good clean out before lighting the fire ready to move off the next day. He had been in the fire-box all night. I took the milk onto the stand, then returned to the farm where I told Mick and Joe. They took some convincing that it was true.

'A man can't get into a fire-box, you must be joking,' said Joe. We walked down the garth to have a look, then back to inform the gaffer.

'Well, that's a corker, men, it beats hen racing. I'll see Miss Hunter and Joyce, he will be hunger'd ti death fast i' there all neet.'

Bacon sandwiches and hot tea were passed in to Freddy. With no telephone, Mick had to go by car to Finghall to let Jim Jackson know, but he had gone to work. It was nearly one o'clock when he arrived to take the front off the fire-box. When finally freed and taken to the farm, Freddy stripped off for a good wash, the gaffer gave him some of Mick's old clothes to put on. Freddy became known as the 'Man in the Box'.

Winters in the 40s were very hard, deep snow with severe frosts. One winter I well remember, no milk left the farm for three days, the milk wagon unable to get through, one churn of milk which had been left on the stand was so frozen we were able to take the cream off in frozen lumps to eat. Rabbits died off in hundreds with the deep snow lasting so long, the River Ure was frozen over, foxes and rabbits were able to cross over. The foldyard was full of birds feeding round the pig troughs, even the pig meal used to freeze onto the troughs, boiling water was used to clean the troughs, this gave the birds water. Four horses pulling a wooden snow-plough with two road men sat on it called at the farm, they were the first new faces we had seen for a week. After having lowance in the farm house and a warm up, the gaffer gave them luck money to make tracks for the sheep in the cow pasture. Turnips which were in a big square pie in the Quarry field, were in a block of ice. When the sun came out melting the snow it ran down among the turnips but at night it froze. Picks had to be used to get them out. When frozen like that, only the older animals had them, frozen turnips made young stock blow up. The mangolds and potato pie took no harm, they had been soiled, then hedge cuttings put on top to break the frost.

A wise man is ignorant of things that are not worth knowing.

To keep our low shoes clean when walking to church at Thornton Watlass, strong working boots were put on, carrying the others, changing into the shoes on the road, leaving the boots in the hollow of the tree which we called the 'Letter Box'. After attending church Joe and I walked to Thirn, calling at the Boot and Shoe pub, where Rab who was a good singer would be in full voice singing his favourite song, 'You'll never miss your mother till she's gone.' Next would be Harrold Sadler, dratin out his version of the 'The wander's warning'. No games were played at the pub on Sunday nights, the dart board was taken down, the landlord Frank Croft would never bring the dominoes out. Arriving back at our farm by 9 o'clock, where the big iron kettle had been left on the hob to keep warm for supper, Mick would ask, 'Does any one want a boiled egg?' Six eggs would be put inside the big kettle, then placed on the fire to cook, we did this several times over the years. Most nights there were logs to split for the fire, kindling wood to light the fire brought in, for this we used old rails which were stored in an outside building. All this had to be done after milking at night.

The two hunters and four working horses were to clip, this made them easier to groom and keep clean. The horses were clipped at night after all the other work had been done. It took three nights to clip the horses, then the milking cows were to clip on the right hind leg on each cow, the side where you sat down to milk them. When done, the clipping machine which had to be turned by hand, had to be cleaned and oiled, then put away for another year.

You have to be rich now to live in the country, it's a case of supply and demand. Once it was the poor folk, and the ones who worked on the land.

I was walking back to the farm one Tuesday night after attending the Home Guard when bombs began to drop over Middlesbrough. As I approached Thirn Lane end, the searchlight in Tucker's field went up which made it very light and I was able to see someone walking towards me, so I released the safety catch on my rifle, ready to challenge whoever they were. As they approached I was able to see that it was Rab (Ron Close) who came walking towards me with a box under his arm. I asked him what he was carrying in the shoe box, he told me money as he lifted the lid off. I had never seen so much money before, the box was full of white five pound notes and one pound notes.

Rab was a very frightened man, he thought that his house would be bombed. I persuaded him to walk back with me, telling him he would be far safer in his own house than walking the countryside with all that money. I never told anyone except those in the farm house.

There was one other incident at the end of the war. Rab was in full voice singing his favourite song when an outsider walked into the Boot & Shoe. After a while he made a comment on the way Rab dressed. Rab always wore a tie and a white silk scarf, and he told the man that clothes alone do not make the man. 'I could buy you out any day, show me your money.' This man who was eyed with suspicion took out his wallet, at the same time flashing the gold rings on his fingers, he took out a few pound notes and a five pound note.

'There, match that,' said he.

Rab unbuttoned his top coat, put his hand into a large inside pocket and drew out a large bundle of rolled up notes, probably in the region of £300! With Rab living out of Thirn, George Hunt and Harrold Sadler walked with him to see him safely home.

Soldiers from the Green Howards came to instruct the Home Guard on handling Mills bombs (hand grenades). We were given a detonator to put into one, then pull out the pin, hold it for one minute, then replace the pin. After each man had held one, the Sergeant pulled the pin from one and threw the grenade, shouting, 'Get down!' It never exploded, being a dummy one.

'Do you think that I would let you play with a real one without protection? I will recommend you all for throwing.'

Sunday, 8 a.m. start, army trucks took the Home Guard platoon onto the moors, to a place specially made for throwing grenades. There were trenches with sand bags for protection. An old tank was the target to throw at. Each man had to have an experienced soldier with him. In the tower stood the sergeant who gave instructions, each man had to throw two grenades, the first one had a seven second detonator in, number two a four second detonator in.

'Stand and watch it, if you don't the bloody enemy will throw it back at you!' shouted the sergeant in the tower.

The machine-gun and other heavy guns had to be fired on Bellerby moor. Four were going from Watlass Platoon to use the machine-gun, Bob Moss, Old Drummer, Harold Towler and myself. Being No 2 gunner I had used the gun with Chinese crackers, this was going to be the real thing. Sergeant Moss went with us onto the moor, where all the other platoons were there testing their big guns. What an assortment when they all got together, from heavy machine-guns to others like a Howitzer.

The targets were the same for the machine-guns as the rifles. When the magazine had to be filled, after 50 rounds were put in one had to be missed out, or the full magazine of 300 rounds would soon be spent. Each man had 50 rounds to fire off in small bursts. Old Drummer who had served in the First World War had to use the gun first. There were men all over the moor. Old Drummer got a shell fast which stopped the gun, he failed to engage the safety catch when trying to release the shell and the gun went off, sending some 20 rounds over the moor. He was disqualified at once. Harold Towler said he did not want to use the gun after that. Bob forgot to release his finger in time, his rounds were soon spent. With being used to the gun, for me it was quite simple, squeeze, 1 – 2, let go. I was given the job of emptying the gun.

On one of those still, warm days in October, the Home Guard had to take Leyburn out of enemy hands. Horse boxes and cattle trailers were used as transport. Disembarking at Dolly Bog Woods, we had to make our way across fields to Spennithorne, surprising the men in white coats (umpires) who were standing in the middle of the road.

'Get down, you're under fire,' they shouted.

How were we to know when all was still and very quiet? Lt. Tucker spotted some movement through his binoculars in a small wood. This was where our nights of using cover in the fields came into use. Four of us managed to get behind the enemy, using our 'Chinese crackers' to let them know they had been fired on. Then the argument started as to who fired first, the umpire was called, even he had not seen us get behind them.

'Do that action again, and let us see how it was done,' he said.

Winter nights the Home Guard used the village hall, soldiers came from Catterick and gave us instructions on how to use different weapons, teaching us to hate the very guts of all Germans. We were told about the concentration camps in Germany, and if they got a foothold in England, young men like myself would be taken to Germany and used as slave labour.

Map reading, morse code, lectures on gas attacks, what the Germans might do, the tactics they would use – we were told, never let the enemy know your strength, hit them and melt away, give them no rest day or night, wear them down. All this was talked over when the wind outside was howling. We had frozen feet, there was no heating, only a smoky oil lamp hanging from a hook on the beam.

We had film shows in Bedale Assembly Rooms, known as the 'Picture House'. The room was full of Home Guard members, while soldiers from Catterick stood guard at the entrance.

Winter gave way to spring. One Tuesday night when we were on the village green doing gas drill, two officers came from Catterick Camp. I was called into the village hall.

'What we have to say to you is very secret, you must not tell anyone for your own good. Are you prepared to be a Freedom Fighter? Your reports are very good, you are a single man, it's men like you we are looking for. Think it over. If you are caught by the Germans you will be shot.'

What had I to lose, if the Germans did invade our land I would have to fight them.

'Yes Sir, I will.'

'Good, sign this form, we have ammunition and guns hidden ready for use if need be, we can rely on you.'

Unknown to the others, I had to go each Wednesday night to Lt. Tucker's house where, with two others, I took apart weapons the soldiers brought with them, then put them together, until able to do it blindfold. I also learnt how to use explosives to blow things up, and to live off the land.

11th, North Riding Battalion Home Guard 1942.
Thornton Watlass Platoon

53

The Home Guard were called out early one morning to look for a suspected parachutist. Arthur Simpson came on his bicycle to call us out. After searching the woods, hollows in fields, all farm buildings, then walking through a field of turnips we came across one which had been pulled up with some eaten off it. We knew that a rabbit had not been gnawing on it. After a while we came across an old woman who had lost her memory and had stayed out all night. We found her sitting on the back of the River Ure two miles from home. We saved one life even if we were so intent on destroying another.

I had been on all night guard with two others, through the night the army had been passing our check point. A soldier on a motorcycle was stopped, he told us that a convoy of trucks would be passing. Where they came from, or where they were going, we never knew. The trucks had only pin pricks for the light to show through, to see on the dark twisty roads. We had a friendly wave from the men in the back of them.

When the bombers began to return to Leeming airfield we saw something fall from one. On arriving back at the farm just after 6 a.m., Arthur Simpson called, the Home Guard was needed to look for a piece of aircraft. It was found in Mr Barninham's field at Pond House, a section off the tail, it had to be guarded until the R.A.F. came to collect it.

More hand grenades were to throw, Watlass Home Guard were taken to a quarry near Masham. Each man had two grenades to throw. In the quarry stood a tree, the second man to throw one was told to, 'Get the buggers higher, and away from you.' This he did, the grenade exploded among the branches of the tree. The soldiers who were with us never expected anything like that. They moved us to another part of the quarry. When throwing we had no protection, only lying flat on the ground behind a small hill.

It's twenty past five, Broadwith's men have been up an hour and you lot still ligging i'bed.

May 13th, May Day for the farmers, on that day all stock would be turned out into the fields. A farm hind would leave his job to move to another farm. The trees are in full leaf, the young crows leave their nest.

That evening Joe, Mick, Gill and myself walked to Sand Hill Wood to shoot young crows. About twenty young rooks were shot, sufficient to keep their numbers down. Back at the farm, the young rooks were skinned, only the two legs and breast off each bird was used in making the crow pie which was very good to eat.

'Best lamb is layed dead this morning men, yer'll etta tak less pay or work an hour longer each night to pay for it. Ah's gihan to be begged, Broadwith never as any dead lambs, ours get over well fed, yer'll 'etta give 'em less.'

'Aye,' said Mick, 'then we will be like Denison, War-Ag turned him off for bad farming, he bought a bull and buried it the same week.'

That would be the usual talk around the dinner table, when Mick and his father would argue it out over different things. Dinner would be roast beef or lamb, followed by boiled 'spotted dick' pudding.

'Ray Musgrave is coming this afternoon to sow maiden seeds in yon field of barley at Mooser. Yer'll 'etta have your skates on men, ti keep up wi him, he's the only good seed sower that I know of round here.'

'Maiden seeds' were clover seeds for a two year ley.

Ray Musgrave put the seed on by finger and thumb, out of an old bread tin, with the help of two markers and following the drill brede. The maiden seeds, as they were called, were put on at twenty pounds to the acre, they were under sown in barley when about three inches high, then rolled in with the Cambridge roller.

During the blackout some nights were very dark. It was one such night when I was at the Buck Inn at Thornton Watlass; Rabbit (Ron Close) the local scrap dealer was there. Rab made the mistake of telling everyone that he would walk through the churchyard to cut the corner off when walking home to Thirn.

'I'm not frightened,' said Rab.

Unknown to Rab, Bill Wake and Sid Hunt slipped out of the pub before he set off for home. They went into Frank Allinson's stable for a trace chain, then into the church for a white surplice. Sid Hunt hid behind a yew tree with the chain, Bill Wake with the white surplice on stood in a newly dug grave. When Rab came along, Bill Wake rose slowly up, asking, 'What time is it mate?'

At the same time Sid rattled the chain. Rab ran back to the pub speechless.

If Candlemass be fair and bright, winter will have a second flight. If Candlemass be dull with rain, winter will not come again.

'You want two load of hay in this morning men, an gan careful with it, we owt to have half of it left, it's nobbut half way through winter. Me and our George are going to Bedale seein ez it's Tuesday.'

Two horses were yoked into the carts, shelvings put on, two forks, hay spade, ropes and a stee (ladder). The stack we went to was in Campbell Field. It had been fenced round with sheep netting, a hurdle used as a gate. First the right amount of thatch had to be taken off, the band fastening it on had to be rolled onto a stack stob for using again. While I did this Joe was busy sharpening the hay spade with a bullstone, then using the stee, he climbed onto the stack top and cut a dess from the middle of the stack to the outside, which was around 3 feet square. The top hay was called 'Stot hay', this was thrown onto the ground, this and the stack bottom were put on the last load.

A dess of hay was cut, but a stamp of hay was taken off to put on the cart. If cut right and not chiggled, you got a lovely load of hay. The two loads were to rope down then taken to Grange farm, where Joyce brought out the lowance – a mug of tea, warm jam pasty and tea cake. One stall in the stable had to be filled with good hay, the rest taken into the barn, unloaded by hand and stacked up.

Meantime, Gill and Mick had turned out all the stock to drink, bedded up, fed the sheep and the lambs on the brek. Joe and I had to go and clean up round the hay stack, taking the old thatch to Mooser for bedding. We gave Gill a hand to chop the turnips which had to be turned by hand. While the 30 young beast were out drinking, 20 skeps full of turnips are carried, then the old thatch used for bedding them up. The two carts were then loaded with barley straw which is in battens. 70 battens were put onto each cart, this enabled the load to go under the barn roof at the Grange. All this had to be unloaded before dinner.

After listening to the one o'clock news I had to yoke a horse into the cart. Gill and Joe gave a hand to lift the chain-barrows into the cart, the harrow bawk, two swingle-trees and a rock-tree were needed for yoking the horses to the chain-harrows. The grass land was harrowed to knock the cow claps about and the mole hills, it also pulled the dead grass out.

With one horse tied behind the cart I set off for Mooser, which was well over half a mile away. The afternoon was brighter than the morning, there were breaks in the clouds. Around two o'clock I heard an aircraft, one which sounded like a German plane. (The Heinkel bomber was easily recognized by its desynchronised engine which gave it an uneven beat.) Sure enough, over the field that I was chain-harrowing flew a Nazi plane, flying low, the markings were clearly seen when it passed from one cloud to the other. It passed over Bedale where a Spitfire caught up to it and fired at it. (The Nazi plane was reported to have come down near Redcar.) Mick, along with many more, witnessed it being hit and they all cheered.

At tea that night it was well talked about, the gaffer thought that they might have photographed the farm. (That same night the Germans tried to bomb Leeming air field, but their bombs fell near the village of Scruton.) After milking, the others came into the stable, sitting on the corn bin, it seemed more snug in the stable than the cow byre. We talked about the weather, what work to do the next day, whether there was a Social Evening near at hand. Seven o'clock we went into the farm house, where each one in turn washed at the sink in the back kitchen, the stable lamps being lit for light and warmth.

Mick busied himself putting the newly charged accumulator, which he had brought back from Bedale, onto the wireless which stood on the windowsill for it needed an aerial and earth wire. After listening to the nine o'clock news, we then listened to Lord Haw-Haw with the German news in English, boasting about how soon they would be having Christmas dinner in London. We played draughts while listening to him. If the gaffer wanted a game of dominoes, four of us would play; Gill would be reading, Miss Hunter darning socks, so Joyce who was a good player made up the four hand. Some games caused quite a stir, arguing as to who won the last game. 'Now ar'll tell you what,' said the gaffer, 'Yer yan apiece an ar's two – how's that?'

'Nay be buggered,' said Mick, 'we 'evn't had that many games, so come off it.'

'Just like you, our George, thoo can't count right, if you had some yows of thee own, thoo wadn't be able ti count 'em right, and another thing our George, give over sweearing, you are always at it.'

57

*By you do tak some shifting ev a morning, you want my bed ti lig on
for a change.*

'My boots were never cold when I was like you chaps, they weren't off
me feet lang enough ti gan cold. Ah nivver had any need far a jacket, I
were always too thrang to put one on. Ah never had time ti gan ti church
like you lot, yer get ower much time off these days, I saved me brass ti
start farmin, not like you lot, spend it in Croft's. In the morning, two on
yer had better give Mrs Abbot a day's threshing.'

That meant Joe and I. Sid Abbot was a good stacker, he always made
a round stack which started off on a cart wheel, the eight stacks were a
picture to look at. Sand Hill was a bleak and windy place, situated on a
hill top. Wherever Joe and I went to thresh, we always took our sack
hoist to lift the 16st sacks of barley up to enable us to carry them,
without it they were to lift onto a barrel, then you had to bend down to
get under the sack to carry away. Sid Abbot had got a new J.A.P. engine
fitted up for chopping turnips. He had a gangly sort of a lad working for
him, one who would fall over his own shadow, one who always had a
muffler round his neck, a cold sort of a youth, frightened to take his
jacket off. He would show us all what the engine on the turnip chopper
was for, when starting it up his muffler got caught in the fly-wheel when
it started, pulling him down on to the engine. If we had not been there, it
would have choked him. Sid took the muffler off him and told him,
'Waken thee sen up, or thoo'll waken up to find thee sen dead one day.'

'Thoo mun have the afternoon off, Chisum, it's Setterday, our Joe
will finish yon drilling, thoo'll etta ev some holidus if we can spare thee.'

Joe was drilling oats in the Quarry field and when turning, the pole
broke.

'Well, that's a corker, beats hen racing, yer'll etta get it mendid
before munda, whatever were you doing our Joe? It's not like you to do
that with implements.' So it was to Ostler Brass Wood to select a larch
tree, cut it down, square it off at one end to fit into the corn drill, then fit
the cross piece ready for Monday morning, all done by hand on the
Saturday night.

When the grass is dry at morning light, look for rain before the night.

When cutting grass for hay, I started as dawn was breaking. The grass damp with dew cuts better, and it was also cooler for the two horses. When the sun came up and dried the grass, wild flowers opened out, the moths and flies that came off them did not rise up very far, swallows came low feeding off them, following the cutter round. The moths were small and of many colours. When the horses stopped unexpected there were blood sucking clegs to be killed; the warmer the horses got, the more the clegs came to annoy them. A cleg can rest on a human, you would never know until it bites, it's like someone touching the back of your neck with a lit cigarette.

Campbell Field that I used to cut was full of beautiful wild flowers, it was called 'Old land hay'. It was the last field to be cut, to enable the flowers to seed. Young pheasants and partridge were to drive out of the standing grass, some were so small one never knew if they all went out to hide under the new cut swathe, out of the way of the sparrow hawks. When cutting, field mice ran about, they were soon picked up by the hawks which hovered persistently overhead, they were not afraid of the machine and horses.

In the heat of the summer months the flies were unbearable at times, especially when it was like thunder, with not a breath of fresh air. A red-spotted handkerchief was tied round your neck to stop hay-seeds falling down and sticking to your sweating skin when forking hay to make pikes, the dust and sweat made you itch and scratch.

It was lovely when the time came to walk down to the river, the four of us each with a towel, stripped off, jumped into the river, we had no bathing costumes to put on. We were not alone, there were other farm lads to see higher up the river. It was 10 p.m. by the clock, the sun still shining, but only eight p.m. by the sun.

Working days were long with two hours on the clock, when the cows were brought in to milk, thousands of flies came into the byre. When milking by hand you were pestered with flies, sweat dripped off your face with the warmth off the sun drenched cows who lashed their tails to and fro to dislodge the flies which were sucking their blood. The milk which had been taken onto the stand was returned the next day, it was sour, the water in the horse trough being too warm to cool it.

If I were you lot, I'd tak me bed ti Croft's an sleep on it there for the night, for what good you are on a morning, you won't get up.

It was early October 1944 when three Italian prisoners of war came to work at the Grange Farm. They came in an Army truck from the Prisoner of War Camp at Cowling. As they walked up to the farm house, each man carried a parcel which they offered to us saying, 'Manjaree' (food). There were two cheese sandwiches wrapped in newspaper which was their midday meal. The gaffer came out to see them, looking at the sandwiches he said, 'They can't eat that and be expected to work on it, arl see Miss Hunter and Joyce.' When the gaffer came out, he told us to throw the sandwiches to the pigs over the foldyard gate. What a look on their faces when they saw what we had done.

'Yer mun ev some dinner wi us, yer can ev a bacon sandwich an' a mug of tea now, ti put somemut inside yer. Ah ween't ev it said that I mistreated someone's sons miles away frev yam.'

Can you imagine any one talking to a foreigner in dialect for them to understand. We had a difficult time trying to get them to understand they would be having dinner in the farm house. 'Thoo'll be working wi'em, Dennis, get em ti understand what I mean, it'll be thy job at night ti sign their work sheet.'

Their eyes lit up when lowance was brought to the field where we were picking potatoes. 'Me Ginarto, you very good here,' he said in broken English, he was the spokesman for the other two.

For the first three days they came in the army truck, after that by bicycle. At meal times they had the same as we had, sitting at a small round table. Each morning they came to work, the gaffer gave them a packet of ten Woodbines each, a mug of tea with a bacon sandwich.

We found them very helpful, they would work on their own. Ginarto was a very good worker, his parents were farmers in the Po Valley; Bruchtette had been a student in Rome, he was more playful; Geanio, his parents had shops, he was not cut out for land work, but did his best.

Over the months I taught them English, they were teaching me Italian, I asked them how they were captured. 'No capture, we walk to the British when in Africa.' They had a book, 'Italian-English.' The problem was the words that we used were not in the book, such words as 'larl', for little. What do you tell them when they asked, 'Dennis, what is a bugger?' There were no swear words in the book. Each prisoner had an army uniform on which was the colour deep purple with a yellow circle on the back, on the right trouser leg was a triangle in yellow.

Life is just one dammed thing after another.

Mrs Spink took a turn for the worse and was not expected to live. Harvest came to a standstill, the drive from the cart track to the farm house had to be cleaned off, mow the nettles in the orchard, weed the front garden, clean out the privy, then white-wash the inside to make it smell sweeter.

Wally Auton from Thornton Watlass came that night to take the honey from the four bee hives in the back orchard before taking them onto the moors. The next day we were leading corn to a stack which was being made at the back of the house near the pond. Joe was stacking, Joyce was his picker, I was forking the loads off. It was around 6 p.m. Miss Hunter came shouting, 'Come quick, the bees are stinging your father.'

Running into the house we found the gaffer under the sofa trying to get away from the bees. We had to lift the sofa off him, the bees were still on him.

'Close the door,' shouted Joe, 'I want every bee in this house killing, they might have done the old man in.' The gaffer's face was beginning to swell, the top of his head and his arms were all bee stings.

All there was to put on the stings was the 'blue bag' which was used on wash days. As the gaffer sat on a chair his eyes closed with the swelling. No one thought of taking him to the doctor.

It had happened while the gaffer was taking two large meat dishes with honey on, to stand in front of the hives for the bees to take back the honey, then the bees attacked him.

We had more bee trouble when they were being taken by car to Ellingstring near Masham onto the moor for heather honey. They had been fastened in the night before, using plough cords to stop the hives from falling apart, also to carry them with.

After tea three of us put one hive in the back of the car and one on the carrying rack at the back. Joe volunteered to sit on the back seat with the bees. Near Killgrim Bridge (so called, because a dog named Grim was drowned, after a curse had been put on the bridge) Joe got stung, the bees were getting out. Mick wanted to throw the 'bloody lot' into the river and the other two hives left at home with them.

We did manage to stop them escaping and continued on to Ellingstring to a farmer called Croft. I well remember the long line of hives behind a wall, probably up to sixty.

You lot want less food. Miss Hunter feeds you ower well, if you were hungry, you'd get up for breakfast, not lig i'bed so long.

From October to the end of March, once a fortnight in Watlass Village Hall there was a Social Evening, playing games and dancing, even the soldiers from the searchlight joined in. Social Evenings were in aid of the Spitfire Fund, Welcome Home Fund. It was at one Social Evening that I met my wife Betty, a young girl with auburn hair, and I plucked up courage to ask for a dance. Gill told me that he used to go to school with her.

'We'll a'e dipped this morning men, put some bloom on yon lambs before they gan ti Masham sheep sales.'

Sheep were dipped at Stan Trewhitt's, Spink had no dipping trough. Lowance was brought out when dipping, and who should bring it out but the young girl I had met at the Social Evening. When the tray with mugs was to take back, Mick and Joe gave me the job, saying, 'Now's your chance, don't let it slip.' From then on Betty and I went out together.

When leaving Plump House to go to Rookwith Grange, some nights in the blackout were very dark. Twice I got lost cycling over the fields, the first time there was no moon, it was very dark. I thought that I was doing fine following the cart track until I ran into a cow which was laid down, falling right over it to the other side. Who got the biggest shock I would not know, I had to walk with the bike until I found a landmark which was an ash tree. The second time it was foggy, walking and pushing the bike, I thought was heading for the farm. I came across the wood fence. I had been walking left all the time, it took well over an hour for a ten minutes' ride. On such nights there was not a sound to be heard, the silence was quite eerie.

An oil lamp stood on the kitchen table, that and light from the warm fire was all we had when playing cards, draughts and dominoes. Two prodded mats were made for the farmhouse kitchen in the long winter nights. Hessian, stretched onto a wooden frame, had a pattern put on to it drawing round a dinner plate. Old clothes were cut up to make the clips, each mat would be five feet long by two feet six inches wide.

Gas attack drill had been carried out many times on the village green. Sergeant Moss carried a hand rattle, one that had to be swung round and round, one never knew when it was going to be used.

Marching with a gas mask on was very unpleasant, no lifting the mask off the face when marching, it had to be treated as the real thing.

Leaving the village green, the H.G marched down the Snape road to Bell's at Watlass Moor Farm, there we had a rest, taking the gas masks off. We had a look around their stock, then masks on again, marching to Dyson's farm at Gebdykes, for a look around their stock and buildings. Gas masks on, then marching back to Watlass by way of Clifton, to Thirn Lane Ends.

The Home Guard was going to be put through a test at Catterick Camp. A Sergeant of the Green Howards gave a pep talk on how to walk slowly through the gas chamber, to give us confidence in our respirators. Respirators were fitted on outside, on entering a room the door was closed, then we walked through some rubber curtains into a long narrow passage, stopping for a while to give us confidence in the respirator, through some more rubber curtains into a room, where the door opened into fresh air.

The H.G. had to learn map reading, with the Easterly's and Westerly's. Summer nights a grid reference of supposed parachutists would be given, which generally turned out to be a small wood which was soon surrounded by Snape and Watlass H.G.

Sunday morning, Bellerby Moors for map reading. As usual an 8 a.m. start from Watlass, we were taken onto the moor where there was not a tree in sight, only miles of moor land. Each platoon was given a different map reference. Lt. Tucker and Lt. Skidmore (Snape) studied the map, after a careful study, we set off carrying full pack across the moor.

After much grumbling Sergeant Moss asked to see the map reference. We were going the wrong way but try to convince the two in charge! They never put into practice what we had been taught about the observation of the countryside. The grid reference took us to the N.A.F.F.I in Catterick, we were late.

Arthur Simpson the postman brought news, when he came with the letters, of what other farmers were doing, such as when they started haytime or harvest, who had killed a pig and what weight it was, when they were going to thresh and wanted a borrowed man, he also carried cigarettes for sale.

Folk then were more kind and helpful, a lot of bartering went on, such as the loan of a man to pay for seed corn, or a load of mangolds or hay. I have cut grass on small holdings in exchange for their help.

The more grass land that was ploughed out, the less there was for the stock, they were being pushed into smaller space and were constantly breaking down fences into the corn fields.

What with stock straying, rabbits eating acres off, some corn fields only had half a crop on. Evenings, when we had the chance, were spent walking round the boundary fences looking for gaps where the sheep had broken through. For fencing wood, trees were cut down in Ostler Brass wood. Jim Jackson came with his saw bench to make rails, stakes and logs. Wild life was plentiful, such as linnets, goldfinch, chaffinch, and rabbits ran about in thousands.

The first field to be harvested had to be skimmed over with the plough then mustard and rape drilled on with a fiddle drill. In October the sheep and lambs were put onto it.

Joss Shaw, who was a retired farm worker, gave a hand on the farm while we were busy soiling the mangold pie. Old Joss was giving a hand one day when, sitting down for lowance, he said, 'They've gat him, arl say no more.' Joss never mentioned it again, we found out later that his second son had been killed in Italy.

He told me some interesting things of life when he was younger, like the farm lad who was cheeky to his boss, one John Thomas Fenwick who farmed at Marriforth. He tied the lad to the cart wheel then drove across the field. Also that the little cottage he lived in at Rookwith had been a public house and a place for changing horses when coaches were in use.

As the evenings got darker at the end of October there was a 'back-end' feeling in the air, owls began to hoot out, occasionally a mating fox would be heard in the fields at the back of the farm house.

Grange Farm was somewhat lonesome in winter when the lane winding its way to Rookwith was impassable with snowdrifts, the trees around the pond all still and silent, capped with snow.

When the day's work was done we sat round the blazing fire, Miss Hunter darning socks, while four would be prodding a mat for the kitchen floor, listening to the gaffer telling tales of when he was a lad.

'Midges, you lot don't know what midges are, I were yance fencing yar neet, it were just about sunset, ar'd left me crowbar behind, when I went to pick it up, the midges flew away with it.'

'Ah yance went to feed some poultry wi Indi corn, the last lot Ah threw out, a gold sovereign dropped on ti't grund. Ah picked it up, put it in me pocket, Ah were that chufft wi me sen, Ah turned a cart wheel. The sovereign fell out of me pocket, down a crack in't grund, so Ah put the bucket ower it, then went yam for a spade, dug all day and neet. But Ah nivver fun it, that's why ar's so poor today.'

'Noo, Ah'll tell yer wat men, fost tahm Ah went ti Leyburn by train, I had ti walk ti Jervo station, Ah wanted a new calved coo, and ti see Sam Turner. I ed ti gan an see a fella sat at the back of a desk, and he asked mer, "Wheea are yer gahin?" "Thats my business none o'thine". Sez he, "Ah caan't gi'e yer a ticket if Ah deean't know where yer gahin". So Ah tell't him Leyburn, ti buy a coo an ti see Sam Turner, Sez he, "Ah deean't want ti know all't history." So Ah tell't him, "Thoo seemed inquisitive aboot it." "There's thee ticket, yan and fow'pence, an deean't loose it." Fost thing Ah see'd when it set off were a chetch run across a field, next minit some coos and a man flew past, then a hay stack flew past that quick yer c'u'dn't keep yer ee's on't. That's fost and last tahm for me on a train.'

'Before I was your age, I worked on a farm on't wolds, where there was fowerteen 'oss men. When gihan in for breekus ya morning, Ah tripped ower me boot lace. Ah nivver had tahm ti fasten it, you blokes always ev plenty of tahm. When I picked me sen up, they were all coming out fra breekus, so I had to turn round an gan wi'em to work, ti how (hoe) turnips. Foreman had never been past before when howing, so I gat in behind him, and I passed him. When he got to the row end, he was that mad wi hissen, he layed down an ficked his boot soles off.'

'I were that good at slashing hedges, the boss used ti tak mer ti slash in a tub trap. Ah could slash that far in one day it took me two days to walk back yam, an you lot talk about work, you don't know what work is, and when it came ti huggin corn—'
'Oh, shut up!' said Mick.

If a naked woman was running around outside, you lot wadn't get up ti ev a look, so get up just for once men.

The weather had been fine and dry through August into September, Joe and I were well ahead of the stookers with bindering. The next morning it was raining, when at breakfast the gaffer gave his verdict.
'It's gihan to be a wet day men, you mun all gan to stook, wet or fine, it wont hurt you to get wet for once, get some of that dust off yer. If I'd

Opening oats out, (Courtesy: Mr G. Tilsbury Marton)

66

been stooking it would have all abeen deean, Ah couldn't sleep wi all yon lot ti stook up, you lot will lig in bed ower lang ev a morning. I think ower much about you,that's why I let you stay, but I'll tell you what, if you all gan ti stook, when you get done you can ev the rest of the day off, how's that?'

With old trousers on, no shirt, an old jacket and cap, we set off to stook the two fields which would be about 20 acres.

The four of us Joe, Mick, Gill and myself, each man taking three rows of sheaves, that's twelve rows going round the field.

When the sheaves were picked up properly it saved a lot of walking, the stooks were set to catch the midday sun. This was the first day we did without lowance, it was too wet to expect anyone to bring it out. We were soon soaked to the skin but it was warm, we had the two fields stooked by dinner time. Before sitting down to dinner we had all been washed and dry clean clothes on.

'Hi-ya done men, and what are you gihan to do this afternoon?'

'Keep you to your word and have the rest of the day off.'

'By god men, I've slippt up there. If I'd known you wad get done, I would have come with you, and had the rest of the day off with you, but I suppose I'll have to stop at home and look after the farm.'

After dinner the old coats and trousers were put through the wooden roller mangle, then hung up in the stable to dry. Mick got the Austin 12 car out. It was still raining when we went to Croft's, the pub was supposed to close at 2 o'clock but when Mrs Croft locked the door there were six soldiers and four from the farm to play darts and dominoes.

'Have you been in Croft's all afternoon men, if I were you I'd tak me bed there an lig on it for what you lot think of the farm. You might have stayed at yam and cleaned a box or two out ti save time after harvest, but you lot have plenty of time ti spare, arl bet Broadwith and his men were at work all day, they don't gan rushing ti spend their brass in Croft's.'

One hour's sleep before midnight, is worth two after.

As the sun was setting, bombers from Leeming were taking off for another raid over Germany. They passed over the farm house groaning under the weight of bombs, the farm house shook and vibrated as they circled to gain height, others from the west were passing over high up.

It was time for me to go on all night guard from 10 p.m until 6 a.m. It never seemed to be dark for very long in midsummer, I can assure you that the nights were far from being quiet; birds, especially the curlews and plovers, called out all night, they were good watch dogs.

Standing under a tree, I have seen many a fox pass by, whether they knew I was standing there I never could tell. It was surprising how the plovers gave advance warning from field to field until the fox came into the field where I was. There were four hen huts in the field, one which was used by the H.G. the fox avoided, but would go round the ones with hens in.

As dawn was breaking the bombers returned, from an advantage point I had a good commanding view of Leeming aerodrome and was able to see them approach for landing. Each morning a light on the Hambleton Hills would start flashing out a signal, -. – C, then a different letter another morning. Some planes came overhead, then the searchlight in Tucker's field would go up onto the plane, then swing the light in the direction of Leeming. When Middlesbrough or Hartlepool was being bombed, all the searchlights around went up, with each rumble of bombs the cock pheasants shouted out.

A young man came to work for Curzen Howe Herrick, at Clifton Castle. He joined Watlass Home Guard. Where he came from or what he was I never found out, the only thing that I knew was that he was no good for anyone. We were going onto the rifle range and it was his second Sunday with the H.G, he also carried a rifle. On the range he stood between Bob Moss and myself. It wasn't until I heard Bob shout, 'Fire the bloody thing!' that I looked at him. He was looking away from the target, his rifle laid on the ground. He never did fire the rifle. After being questioned, we found out that he was a conscientious objector; no one wanted to know him after that, he left and we never saw him again.

How-ay men, sun will soon be up, are you going to lig there till it burns yer ee's out.

'Can thoo kill a lamb, Chisum?' said the gaffer when having breakfast.

'I can if you want to save it from dying,' I said.

'Good, thoo and our George will etta kill one, Stanley, Broadwith and Mrs Abbot will want some.' This was the first of many, how were we to know when the Germans would invade our land? There were no fridges to keep meat fresh, it was to share among the other farmers.

'Ah would get some Land Girls ti help out, but if I did you lot would nivver leave them alone, and besides, you want nowt we lasses fra Leeds, they don't no how ti cook and bake like Miss Hunter here.'

'Broadwith tells ma there's a clay pigeon shoot on at Thirn in Loadman's field, I'll be off with yer, ti show you all how to shoot, an tak't fost prize off yer, then what will you say to that?'

'Ah seed young Hunt, he's ez narra ez a hen between t' ee's, he leeaks arrish ti deeath, not unless he ezent had enough ti eat, he's yan of the best to play darts in Croft's. I aim ti gan ti Masham sheep sales ti morn an't day after if our George will tak us, he's ower fond of wasting his brass i' Croft's. Our Joe and you are always at work, I'd like you both ti ev some time off when we get worked up.'

'We want a calf sorting out fo't auction sale at Watlass, fo't Welcome Home Fund. We mun tak care of't soldiers coming home, they will have had a hard time of it, not like you blokes been able ti lig i' bed of a morning, and fed on the best and nowt to show for it. If some of them soldiers ed been here in your place we would have been worked up.'

'Yer mun get done in good time in t' morning men, there's a ploughing demonstration on at Gebdykes, it will be a collar and tie job. Wor-ag is gihan ti show us how it's deean, not that they can we men like Woodbine Willy working fo 'em, they only dee a bit of rough work fo't farmers. It's queer how some of them blokes that come round to tell you how to farm, an mak brass, have been turned off theirs for bad farming, but then we can all spend someone else's brass. It will be starvation stood watching men, so put a good top coat on.'

69

The value of life lies, not in the length of days, but in the use we make of them.

September, a lovely mellow time of the year, plums had to be picked for bottling and jam making, bramm'ls were to pick off the hedgerows, this had to be done at night after work, when we had the time.

All the stooks had been led into stacks which were made out in the fields in case of fire. Hen huts with cock chickens in were taken onto the stubble fields to clean the loose corn up. Each night near sunset, they were to let out to stubble and watch over, to see they did not stray far from the huts. The two farm dogs seemed to know and helped keep the chickens near the huts.

Apples were to pick, they were laid in rows in the large room up the back stairs, pears picked, then stored in wooden boxes with oat chaff between them.

All stacks had to be thatched, stack-stobs had to be cut from the hazels in Ostler Brass wood. Battons of wheat straw were to draw, (that is to take the long straws out for thatching, the other going for bedding.) The long straw was put into bundles called a 'threve', next water from a watering can was put over them, this made the straw lay flat on the stack, also stopped it from slipping and blowing about when thatching.

Joe and I did the thatching, both on the same stack, shears used for clipping sheep were used to cut the ends of straw level along the stack-side. When thatching a hay stack, the sides and ends had to be pulled (called ploating). This gave the stack a good clean look. After the stacks had been thatched, four of hay and up to twelve of corn, the eight acres of potatoes were to pick. A load of wheat straw was taken where the potatoes were going to be pied. Four extra helpers were all that we were able to get for potato picking. Each night the day's picking had to be covered over with straw and spotted. (A spade full of soil put on here and there to hold the straw on.) When all the potatoes had been picked, the pie or clamp had to be soiled over. Next the potato field was harrowed, the tops cleaned off, then drilled with back-end wheat. The mangolds were next, they had to be cleaned and pied and soiled over.

When a strong west wind brings thick cloud scudding across the sky, then comes the rain, for a while one does not mind, work had to go on, muck to be led out. To keep dry, a hessian sack was made into a 'Pixie hood' placed on the head, tied round the waist with 'billy band' (string). A thick cotton cake sack was put over the horse's back behind the saddle, to help keep the horse dry from the penetrating rain driven by the strong wind.

Furrows of repentance are plowed i' youth, and sow'd wi t' seeds o' pleasure, but harvest 'ez ti be reaped with a blunt sickle when yan's back is bent and gitten past work.

'Yer mun gi' yon land which is for roots a good mucking, it wants fowerteen leeads ti't yakker, ti dee onny good.'

It was my job to team the carts, a muck drag was used for this, three horses and carts were used when leading muck out, the carts were filled by the three Italian prisoners and Joe brought the full loads to the field. The heaps were made 7 yards apart each way then spread manually with a gripe. When this was being done, starlings came to feed off it in their thousands. As night approached they gathered into huge flocks, some so big they were like a cloud passing over. Somewhere around 112 loads of muck would be put onto eight acres, after the bulk of muck had been spread, I went to plough with the Fordson tractor, wet and fine. I have been so cold I have stopped the plough to run about and get warmed up.

Despite all this hard work we still had to attend the Home Guard.

November, the fat pig had to be killed, the police had to be notified when killing one, a permit was needed to kill one pig.

The copper fire had to be lit, hot water was used for scraping the pig. Billy Wilk came to do the job, two pigs were killed on one permit. The men from the Ministry were always snooping around the farms but the man under the cloth cap, and straw in his mouth was cleverer than he was, or ever would be. I have seen an outside 'privvy' all done out, under the lid, two pigs laid down in salt.

When snagging turnips, four rows had to be left every so far across the field, then when the turnips had been led off, lambs were put on in a brek, which was made with sheep netting, to fatten up for market. Brewers grain was brought from Theakston of Masham. When wet, if a lamb ate too much it made it drunk, they used to stagger about.

When the ground is frozen the turnip leaves are white with frost. With no gloves to put on, you had to take hold of the turnip, cut the root off, then the leaves, praying that the sun would soon shine to melt the frost. Sheep wool was put inside our boots to keep feet warm while snagging. To keep our hands from being chapped they were rubbed with fat bacon from the breakfast table each morning; boots were rubbed over with harness oil, to keep water out. The morning was made brighter when the fox hounds came onto the farm land. We followed them for well over an hour, this warmed you up, the gaffer did not mind as we got no holidays. We used to stand and talk to our neighbouring farmers and their men.

We were not like the farm lad who was told to hoe turnips while his boss went to market. Next day they went to hoe, seeing that the lad had done very little, he asked him what he had been doing. He replied, 'I've done more than the man over the hedge on the next farm, he's done nothing.'

'And how do you know that?' asked the farmer.

'Because I have been stood watching him all day.'

When ploughing with the spade lug tractor, once started it was never stopped until the day's work was done, this was to save petrol for use in the car. One such occasion in spring, Joe, Mick and Gill had been cleaning the potato pie bottom off then burning the old straw which had covered the potatoes. I had been chip harrowing for barley. I passed them when taking the tractor to be filled with T.V.O. The shed with the tank in stood near the gate into the 30 acre field where they were working. Behind the shed stood a large wheat straw stack. After filling up I drove the tractor some way back to meet them, then walked with them to the farm for dinner. While we were washing our hands, Miss Hunter shouted, 'The big stack is on fire!'

'It can't be, we've just left it,' said Joe.

We ran down the paddock, the T.V.O. tank was on fire which held 200 gallons. The hedge, gate and the big straw stack were all ablaze. All we were able to do without any water was to try and contain the fire and save the hedges. Spink was the only one then with a tractor so we were unable to borrow any T.V.O. (Tractor Vaporizing Oil).

The insurance paid for the damage, which amounted to £27.0.0. which was for one gate, tank of T.V.O. and the straw stack. Straw then was plentiful, you could not give it away, the fire was the talk of the neighbourhood, something fresh to talk about.

When riddling potatoes, the riddle had to be turned by hand. Eight tons were put up to make a load, the potatoes all went to Bradford. One wagon which came for a load brought with it some 'shoddy' from the woollen mills, it was all to unload by hand. It consisted of flock rubbish, buttons, etc., no feed value whatsoever for the land, that was the only load that came.

The gaffer's verdict, 'You might ez well lig i' bed men ez play on wi' that lot, because that's what you like ti dee.'

If Hitler gets here, you blokes wont be able ti lig i'bed of a morning, so mak the most of it now while I'm in charge, and think a bit about yer.

It was one of those mornings in harvest when there was a heavy dew. The barley that had to be cut was under sown with clover, we had to wait for it drying out before starting to binder.

The canvases on the binder had to be dry for them to work properly; to fill time in, we were cutting thistles with a scythe each at Mooser. While I was sharpening the scythe, the first finger on my right hand went down the scythe blade, cutting it to expose the knuckle.

There was no First Aid box, no sticking-plaster, the farm dog licked it clean, then Mick found a fuzz-ball, sometimes called a puff-ball, this was placed over the knuckle, then tied in place with handkerchief until midday. At the farm house it was bandaged up with a piece off an old pillow case, which was used for such occasions.

I still have the scar on my finger to remind me of that day.

The turnip chopper was belt-driven by a small petrol engine, it was dangerous to push the turnips down when they were stuck, we used a piece off a fork shaft for this. One morning when Mick was using the turnip chopper he used his hand to release the turnips, when he pulled his hand out the thumb nail on his left hand was missing.

It was bandaged up using the salve out of the cattle medicine chest and bandage off the pillow case. No one thought of going to the doctors in those days.

A peck of March dust and a shower in May,
makes the corn green, and the meadows all gay.

Eight acres had been ploughed out of a pasture field near the river Ure. It had been drilled in oats, rabbits lived in the sandy banks of the river in hundreds. When harvest came and the oats were ready for cutting, the gaffer wanted as many guns as possible in the field.

In the Boot & Shoe pub, we let it be known we were going to cut the oats. Long nets were put round the field by the two gamekeepers, to help catch the rabbits and the binder was taken down in the afternoon, there was no need to open the field out, the rabbits had done that.

Seven guns were in the field, no dogs were allowed on account of the guns. One acre of oats would be left when Joe and I gave over bindering, to help drive the rabbits out of the standing corn.

Well over 300 rabbits had been killed by late evening, they were all to bury. At harvest time the markets were flooded with rabbits, you could not give them away. Next morning when Joe and I went to binder the remaining oats, there were still rabbits running out. After stooking the field of oats, Jim Jackson came with his thresher into the middle of the field. With two horses pulling the paddy sweep, I took the stooks to the thresher; for what was got off the field in corn, it had been a waste of time ploughing it out.

'Now this afternoon men, you mun gether a few nuts, you'll not be gahin far, there's no where ti gan, we want some nuts to mak a Christmas cake an ti eat at Christmas.'

Hazel nuts then were plentiful. It was a Saturday afternoon when we went to gather the nuts, three mangold seed bags were soon filled. They were stored in the gun room, in the same room stood the flour bin, round the walls hung top coats which were used in winter.

If Christmas day on a Thursday be, a windy winter we shall see,
Windy weather in each week, hard tempest strong and thick,
The summer shall be good and dry, corn and beast shall multiply.

'It's Christmas men, we'll ev yon nuts brout out ti eat.'
With the two flat irons ready for cracking the nuts, Mick went to fetch

a bag out. 'By god they feel light.' There were small holes in the bag. When the nuts were emptied out, each one had a hole in it. The other two bags were brought out, they were just the same.

'It's a corker, men, beats hen racing, they all can't be empty ar'll nivver ev that.' Not one nut did we have, traps were set to catch the mice.

By god men, I is bad this morning, if I live long eneeaf ar'll likely dee, then you can call it a day farming here, you will soon be bankrupt.

The gaffer and Mick had been to Bedale market. 'I met up with Billy Lancaster frev Ash Bank, in t' Kings Head pub, an' it cost me a whisky, when I asked him what he was eving; Ah slipt up there men. He tells ma his lads are worked up, and looking for work not like you blokes, lig i'bed ower lang ev a morning.

'I would have asked him back for tea, but I thowt you might still be in bed, and I didn't want to show you up. He tells ma his lads can put ten

Percy Corner as Father Christmas, Burrill Institute

tons of potatoes up in a day, not like you blokes, tak two days. He ez some pig potatoes to give away, I wad have some, but I doubt whether you would find time ti gan for'em, you could ev ta'en a few mangols in exchange.

'When Ah left him I went to pay Billy Asquith meat bill, an' there was this here woman stood looking intiv his shop window, an' you'll never believe this men, he came out to tell the woman, 'That's a pig's head you are looking at, madam.'

She replied, 'I know it's a pig's head, but what I want to know, is it beef or mutton?'

'Ah've got some more sheep dip today, ti put some bloom on them shearlings before they gan ti Masham sheep sales. I was going to get half a dozen new hay forks to replace that one you broke, but if Ah did you wad only have more to break. I don't think it's weight of hay you are lifting that's breaking them, it's wi leaning on'em. You want to be very careful, there's many a man been killed wi leaning on a fork, an t'shaft brekkin' wi't man falling on ti't brokken shaft.

'Broadwith was telling me that Wor-ag, is gahin ti organize a nationwide wood pigeon shoot, starting this coming February, and lasting for six weeks ev a Friday night. Wor-ag is gahin ti issue cheap cartridges for the job, so we will etta ev some, that's if you blokes can find time ti go, an' not be running off ti't Home Guard ev a Friday night.'

One lovely sunny day ten acres of clover hay was ready for putting into a stack. 'I'll tell you wat men, Jim Jackson will bale that hay for us, he's laiting work, me an our George will gan an see him,' said the gaffer. This was 11 o'clock in the morning or 9 o'clock by the sun. (We had two hours extra summer time during the war.) Jim Jackson came into the field with a stationary baler. We started at 1 o'clock to bale, this was the first time that I had seen hay baled. The bales which were tied with wire, weighed around 8 to 10 stone each. We had no hooks for using on the bales to pull them about. I swept the hay to the baler while the others fed it in and stacked the bales, Jim looked after the wire.

'By god, men, them's man killers, I'll ev no more of this.' The farm was not equipped for bales as there was no elevator and everything had to be lifted up by hand. Some of our corn stacks were made too big, it took a long while to top them out. Mick would stand on the long ladder while I passed the shaves (sheaves) up to him on a long fork.

You never had to throw corn sheaves about, it knocked too much grain out of them.

> Time and again men plough the fields
> Time and again the harvest will come.
> Everything ripens at its time
> And becomes fruit at its hour.
> What we have done will not be lost to all eternity.

Friday October 20th 1944 was my 21st birthday. After breakfast I had the rest of the day off to go with Mick to Leyburn market.

My youth had been wasted with the war years, no leisure time at weekends, having to work with the sun, which meant working until midnight in midsummer. When I had done all night guard I returned to the farm and never went to bed, just carried on working. In the middle of haytime we worked until nearly dark, having been on the go for 30 hours, resting only at meal times.

In December 1944 the Home Guard was stood down. There was a big parade at Leyburn for the 11th North Riding Battalion of Home Guard. How well I remember having to line up in the station yard, marching up Leyburn, round the Town Hall, then back to the station yard where speeches were made.

With no more H.G. duties this took a lot of pressure off the farmers and their workers. We were once again able to use the Dutch barn, Sundays were spent going to see your neighbour, to look at his crops and stock, even with our farm being well inland there was always someone calling for help or advice on such matters as a cow to calve, the loan of a horse and cart, or a jag of turnips to spare.

Richard Spink was the first farmer near at hand to have a set of three gang rollers. He had to have a permit from the Ministry of Agriculture to buy them, arriving in time for the spring sowing.

What a big difference it made between two horses pulling one roller and a set of three. My first experience of moving the rollers to another field was a failure. It was steep down to the gate into the next field where I had to roll. The rollers pushed the tractor forward, twisting round and catching the gate post. The tractor was unable to push them back over. I had to unyoke them and drive the tractor through the hedge, then pull each roller back with a chain.

That night I fenced the gap up in the hedge, as I was told, 'To pay for your learning.'

Two farm sales took place at Thirn during the war years, of Mr Albert Hunt and Mrs Loadman. We gave Mrs Loadman a hand with the farm implements, which were put in rows across a grass field, turnip chopper, turnip drill, cake crusher, scrubber, dasher, end-over-end churn, (these were bought to mix seed corn with Cerisan when sowing), straw chopper, winnowing machine, all of which have no use today.

The sale started from the granary steps, all the small tools and oddments had been carried into the granary, forks, hay-spade, skeps or swills, buckets, medicine chest, drenching horns, snaggers, slashers, bundles of stack stobs, jobbers and hoes and oddments from the farm house.

When Sale morning arrived, willing hands soon made the Dutch barn into an auction ring, where the livestock was sold, sheep were penned up in small numbers as they would sell better. The auctioneer started with the usual banter.

Richard Spink on his hunting horse, Dolly
Courtesy Mrs J. Spink, Thornton Watlass.

78

'Now here we have a good square cow, with a leg on each corner. What have I bid for her? She has a bag like a swill, a good milker, forty pounds anywhere, thirty-five anywhere, gentlemen, I am selling this cow, not giving it away, forty pounds have I bid.'

Horses, which were sold in guineas (21/-) were trotted up and down the farm yard by the horseman, with ribbon in the mane and tail and sporting a new helter. I have never been sentimental over animals but one wonders where some of the working horses ended up, after giving years of faithful service.

A farm sale is not like any other sale, it is the disposal of a family livelihood, which only farmers and their men will understand.

It was on the next day when we went to collect an implement that we realized what a farm sale meant: the desolate look of the farm, after all the activity before the sale, no noise from animals, the cow-byre and stable silent, all outbuildings empty and still, not even the bark of a dog.

Sunday morning May 1945, Thornton Watlass Home Guard had its last parade, marching from the village to the church for morning service, after which the Home Guard was disbanded.

Tuesday night, all our equipment had to be handed in, soldiers came from Catterick Camp to check each man's equipment against a list. We were able to keep the uniform and boots.

> We who guarded England's Valleys and Fells,
> Remember your loved ones we guarded well,
> Of brave young souls who stood guard all night,
> Then worked all day until midnight,
> We shall raise our heads with pride,
> For England was guarded well by Home Guard.
>
> Den Chisholm.
> May 1995.

May of 1946, Miss Hunter left Richard Spink to get married.

June 14th, I was second hoeing the mangolds before the start of haytime; it was mid-morning when the gaffer came to let us know that Mrs Spink had passed away. 'Give over, men, and tidy up round the farm before funeral day.' Miss Hunter, now Mrs Welch came for two weeks to give Joyce a hand although she had been managing very well.

'You'll be a bearer, Dennis, along with Stanley, John Broadwith and John Gatenby.' (John Gatenby worked for Spink before I took his place.) Joe, Mick, and the gaffer wore black arm bands. It was a sad time for everyone, also the beginning of the breaking up of a happy family.

'I want you lot to keep out of Croft's (Boot & Shoe pub) for two weeks, and that means you, Dennis, show a bit of respect for mother.'

For two weeks no one left the farm, only Mick on the Tuesday to take Mrs Abbot and the farm eggs to Bedale market.

A little dab of powder, a little dab of paint,
makes a woman look just what she aint.

'Ah've gat a young woman from Skelton coming as housekeeper, a bit older than thoo, Dennis, so keep your 'ees off her, sher's more likely to suit Joe than anyone.'

Saturday afternoon Mick took the car to Bedale to meet her off the bus. Out of the car stepped a young black-haired woman with high-heeled shoes on, and her face all powder and lipstick.

At tea that night the gaffer let it be known to her that I was engaged and would soon be married. Miss Brown did not live up to expectations. 'I can't get her out of bed ev a morning, she can't cook like Miss Hunter use ti, she nivver gets the breekus ready. Joyce here as it all ti dee hersen, and by god men sher ez a bad temper. Ah've gat a wrong un there.'

Came the day when the gaffer brought the lowance with a tear in his eyes. 'By god men, shers ta'en t' higg this morning men, thrown all t' things out of the gun room on ti't back lawn in among the apple trees, boots, coats, wellingtons all ower men.'

Joe told his father to look round the stock at Mooser and when he was out of sight, went to give her a good telling off, making her put all the boots and working clothes back into the gun room.

After that episode Joyce left to work for another farmer. Mick was to marry Mary, Joe was courting Jean, they would soon be getting married. The gaffer knowing that I also would soon be getting married, offered to build a house at Mooser for me to move into after the wedding.

Life had gone out of the family household, Miss Brown had caused a different atmosphere. It was not the same at meal times, the house seemed empty after Joyce and Miss Hunter had left, also the loss of Mrs Spink. The end of November I left after working on the farm for six years.

I am still waiting for some holidays.

> Tired I slept on my bed, in the illusion
>   that work had an end.
> In the morning I awoke to find that my
>   garden was full of flowers.

SINGLETON'S

I started work for Arthur Singleton, Pasture House, in December 1946. I had no holiday, going straight from one farm to the other. My wage was £3 a week, starting time 6.30 am. until 5 pm.

1947 was the year of the great storm. Anyone who lived through it will never forget it, especially those who lived out in the country. January of that year was generally mild, February brought exceptionally heavy snow falls, but the worst blizzards came during the first week in March. I thought it was never going to stop snowing, it did not end until the second week in April. The snow came into the farm buildings through every little hole in the roof, every gap in the doors.

We were able to walk anywhere over the frozen compacted snow. A cold north-east wind had blown it into deep drifts, some over 20 feet deep. Betty and I were able to walk from Pasture House to Burrill to see her parents, walking over walls and hedges as if there were none.

Hens then were free range, the huts were to dig out each day, food and water to carry to them. They were never let out as there was nowhere for them to go, the huts being covered with snow.

Sheep in the fields were to find and dig out then bring into the Dutch barn. When the wind did stop blowing it was very still, the snow deadened all sound, an eerie silence took over. The farm buildings were full of birds, thrush, starling, blackbird and many more.

We used to feed them by spreading round corn on the floors of all the buildings such as the cow byre, turnip house and cart shed.

March of that year was intensely cold, the thaw began in April when the temperature rose quickly, it went from winter to summer, there was no spring. As the snow melted it soon became clear to us how many birds had perished, also thousands of rabbits. It is always the same in deep snow, the small birds perish.

On September 20th of that year Betty and I were married at St Gregory's Church Bedale. We had our reception in the Institute at Burrill, then to Morecambe for our honeymoon. This was the first holiday that I had had from leaving school in 1937. A lot of wartime restrictions were still on when we were at Morecambe. The beach was all barbed wire with huge blocks of concrete to stop tanks coming inland, there were no sign-posts at cross-roads. For a ride out to see the countryside, we went on a mystery tour, the driver got lost on the moors and had to keep asking his way back to Morecambe.

Good words cost nothing.

Four council houses were built in Burrill after the war for agricultural workers. They were the first houses to be wired up for electricity.

Mr and Mrs Catterick moved into one and Rob Paternoster lived next door. When electricity was finally brought to the village the four council houses were the only ones to light up. Mr and Mrs Catterick invited Betty and I to see their electric lights, and to have a go at switching them on and off. What a difference from candle light! Not being used to electricity, we were amazed at such bright lights, especially when we went back to paraffin lamps and candles.

After Betty and I had looked round the new council house, we decided to put our name forward for one. It was some time later that Charlie Catterick pointed out to Rob Paternoster that he had a brown patch on his front lawn. He replied, 'Yes, I know, and I know what's done it, t'Missis put leet on before she drew the curtains across, an t'lectric leet shining throu t'window ez burnt it.' Rob Paternoster left Burrill to live at Crakehall, we were then allocated the council house next door to Mr and Mrs Catterick.

In the May of 1950, I started work for Percy Corner at Cowling Hill. The starting time was 7 a.m. until 5 p.m., working a 50 hour week for £5-0-0, lowance each day, also a can of milk, tea when working overtime, potatoes when available.

Percy was like Richard Spink, spoke in dialect, especially when a car stopped, and the driver asking the way. 'Na then, ezta gitten thee sen lost, wats ter want ti know ev a cold morning like this?'

Richard and Mary (his children) were still at school, at weekends they had work to do, such as feeding the hens and cutting the lawns.

Joe Hodgson was the pigman, Frank Taylor the stockman. I had not been working for Percy very long when he sold his last horse and in its place bought a Ferguson tractor for light work, two David Brown tractors were used for working the land.

In one pasture field there was a very steep hill which was called 'Spectacle Hill', When Frank Taylor first used the Ferguson to go around the stock, he drove the tractor down the steep hill, running into the wall at the bottom; the tractor would not move, he had broken the gears.

HOLIDAYS

In 1950, Betty and I had our first long, away holiday, going to Norwich to stay with Betty's sister for a week. The train left Bedale at 8 o'clock in the morning for York, where we had to change trains. The train for Norwich was full, we had to sit in the corridor on the case that we were taking with us, taking it in turns. No one offered Betty or me a seat, we had nothing to drink, there was none on the train. When the train stopped at a large station I would go and buy fruit or what was available on the platform.

The journey took 11 hours, it was 7 o'clock in the evening when we arrived at our destination.

One time during our stay, I was walking in the park nearby enjoying the sunshine when I got talking to a young man, or should I say trying to

First outing to the seaside.

85

have a conversation with him, but neither of us was able to understand much what the other was saying. It was the same when Betty went to the butcher's shop, they had a job to understand each other.

Today, with travel being so fast, and television, the dialect will soon go. It is considered vulgar today to speak in dialect.

Michael our first child was two years old when we went to Norwich for the second time. We were prepared with food and drink, we had a faster train, one with four seats to a table, the train was not crowded.

The Village Institute, Burrill, organized a trip to Redcar, the first after the war had ended. It was talked about for weeks, until then the village folk had not been anywhere. What excitement when the coach came, for the young ones, it was their first visit to the seaside.

I suppose they would be the same as I was when going on the Sunday school trip to Redcar. We played cricket on the sand, made sand castles, paddled in the sea. To me Redcar was not the same, the war years had altered it. When we took Stephen, our second son, to Redcar, we bought him a bucket and spade, soon as he got hold of it he said, 'Let's go home now, Mam.' He had no interest in the sea, all that he wanted was to be home to dig in the garden.

Tak heed, deeant rake about.

The first time that I heard Percy tell anyone off was an Easter Monday. We had fed all the stock outside and the pigs which lived in 'Pig arks'. A sow which the vet had been attending lay dead.

'We'll leave her until tomorrow, then we'll bury her,' said Percy.

As we stood talking in the barn a car came into the yard, out jumped a young man.

'Now then, wat's thoo want this morning?' said Percy.

'Err, there's a pig dead in one of those huts down there, that wants burying.'

'How's thoo know that, young man?'

'I've been having a look at them pigs down there.'

'Just you wait there young man.' Then away Percy went, returning with a spade in his hand. 'There you are, young man, gan and bury it, and bury it deep.'

'Err, I just wanted you to know it was dead, and wanted burying.'

'Are you having the day off young man?'

'Err, yes.'

'So are we, bugger off back to where you have come from, and don't ever come on to my land again snooping about, there are too many like you sticking their nose in where it's not wanted, so bugger off.'

When the young man set off towards his car, Percy just said, 'Bob'.

The big dog went between the man and his car, showing his teeth with a growl. The young man stopped, not knowing what to do.

'Next time young man, that dog will eat you, he just wants thee and another then he will have eaten two today, think yourself very lucky.'

Summer days, old Bob would lie watching the road from behind the gate which was always open. He would lie there for hours, then anyone walking to the farm house for eggs, old Bob would follow them.

When leaving the house, Mrs Corner had to walk with them, if not, the old dog would not let them go.

Richard and I were busy greasing the combine ready for harvest when a man carrying a case came into the yard, he had a turban round his head, old Bob was following behind. 'How-ay, let's watch this,' said Richard. Through a crack in the Dutch barn boards we were able to see the back door. Mrs Corner opened it with the usual, 'Not today, thank you' then closed the door. When the traveller turned to leave, the dog growled showing his teeth. After two attempts to walk away, the traveller had to knock on the door again. Mrs Corner had to walk back to the road telling him not to call again, or next time he may not be so lucky.

Every door may be shut but death's door.

While we were walking across the cow pasture to look round the stock, Capp, the young dog ran forward to get hold of a rabbit. Percy called him back, seeing that the rabbit just hopped about, not knowing which way to go. The rabbit had a swollen head, its eyes were bulging out and unable to see, Myxomatosis had arrived onto the farm.

It was early May 1954, this was the first rabbit that I had seen with the disease, it was put out of its misery.

Each day after that encounter the fields were to go over using a tractor and trailer to gather up the dead ones, some were to 'scaup' (hit on the head with a strong stick). Most of those we had to put out of their misery had had their eyes pecked out with the crows.

Cycling home to East Witton, the road from Killgram Bridge to East Witton was stinking with dead rabbits, vehicles had crushed them to the road. This was by far the worst thing that I had seen done to animals, it was untold suffering for them.

The Landrace boar pig was running out among some cows in calf; each morning they had a 4st bag of cow cake spread out for them, the pig eating his share. A count of the cows found one missing. Richard and I found the cow dead, its stomach was out, the boar pig having ripped its side open.

'Right lads, we'll ev him in an tak the ivory's off him,' said Percy. The pig was taken into the cow-byre where a rope was put round his lower jaw. The pig screaming, and pulling back on the rope was made fast to the rud stake in the cow stall.

Then Percy using a hammer and chisel knocked its two tusks out, telling the pig, 'There, that never hurt you as much as you hurt the cow, I have to be cruel to be kind.'

Don't think you've all the troubles, you've only got your share.

Came the day when Percy bought a hill farm at Snaizeholme above Hawes, with sixty 'Heughed sheep' (belonging to the farm, horn burns and ear marks go with the farm.)

'Reet lads, we'll gan up yonder and have a look round, we'll take dinner for you.' What an isolated place, well inland, about two miles up an old green lane, no electric in the farm house; a barn, cow byre and two boxes made up the farm buildings, a lovely place to go to for peace and quiet. In spring only the bird song broke the silence.

After a good look round we went to visit other farmers near at hand to make ourselves known, also to see their layout for dipping and penning sheep. 'I want the best that I have seen put in up yonder when the dipping trough and pens are made,' said Percy on our way back home. Two tractors with trailers had to be taken up from the Home farm, a distance of thirty-five miles, for leading ready-mixed concrete down the hill to the farm buildings which was very steep. Electricity was brought across fields from the lowland, a very helpful farmer called Billy Burton came to give a hand. He was later to look after the flock of sheep on the fell.

It was not long before the sixty sheep became three hundred. When the flock of sheep were to gather up for clipping or dipping, we worked until they were all done, some nights it would be 9 o'clock before we left Snaizeholme. Before going onto the fell to gather sheep, we always had a good lowance of beef or bacon sandwiches as Percy would say, 'Something inside of you in case you get lost.'

The biggest problem at the back-end of the year was the sudden drop in temperature with the low clouds passing over. When it was cold with drizzle the sheep would hide behind the rocks, they seemed to know which way you were going to walk round the large rocks, three men with four dogs to help, some sheep were always left behind.

Strays which came in with the flock were put through the dipping trough, then put into a separate pen. When we went home they were loaded into the cattle trailer to be taken to Hawes auction mart, where

Three bales of hay for three hundred sheep. Snaizeholme 1963.

89

they would be looked after by the yard man. The pen which they were left in was where farmers went to look for missing sheep.

Red sky in the morning, shepherd's warning.

Each morning Percy came out to see us he always looked at the sky to give us the weather forecast. 'Aye why, crows are on the topmost branches of the dead tree this morning, a sign of good weather.' It was February '63, that Percy came to see us and give the day's orders. 'I've been round the sheep and I don't like the way they are all huddled together, it's gahin ti snow.'

He was right, deep snow came, we had some good falls of snow in the 60s and this was one of them. While it was snowing, we were busy mending sacks for use on the combine. We used glue and bits of old sacking to patch the holes up made by rats and mice. They were put into bundles of 20, then hung on the bawks out of the way of the rats.

Three days had gone by without the sheep at Snaizeholme being fed. At 8 o'clock the next morning after all the stock had been fed, leaving old Joe Hodgson in charge of the farm, we filled the back of the Land Rover with bales of hay, three shovels, a basket of food and flasks of tea. With Percy driving, his son Richard and myself, we set off to take all the hay to the sheep at Snaizeholme.

The Land Rover travelled well until we left the road above Hawes for Snaizeholme, then the trouble started – deep snow blocked the lane to the farm, but we had to struggle on – from leaving Burrill early morning it would be 3 o'clock in the afternoon when the sheep got three bales of hay. We had to carry the hay to the sheep, they would not come to us. On the fell side the snow had been blown level, in some places we walked into snow waist deep – three bales of hay for 300 sheep and it took all day to do it.

Next morning Percy rang the Ministry of Agriculture at Northallerton, asking for hay to be dropped by helicopter, a big yellow one had been flying around. On the other end of the line a voice asked,

'Can you prove that your sheep are dying of hunger?'

Percy: 'What good are a lot of dead sheep to me?'

Min of Ag: 'It costs £90 an hour to keep that copter flying about.'

Percy: 'I'll send you the bill for every yow that dee's up there.'
Min of Ag: 'Well can you prove to us they are dying?'
'Reet lads, we'll etta gan back up yonder and bugger that lot.'
With the back of the Land Rover full of hay bales we arrived at Snaizeholme to find the sheep had been brought down off the fell to the farm and had been given the hay that we had left.

A farmer, Billy Burton, had seen us struggling on, watching through his binoculars the day before, he and his son had brought them off the fell-side.

If t' bull snorts don't linger.

'We'll gan and have a word with Walter, see how he's getting on.'

It was one of those days before haytime started, when we had some time to spare. After leaving Walter, we walked through our foldyard, the big Lincoln Red bull was looking over the bottom half of the byre door.

'He's slippt his chain, we'd better fasten him up,' said Percy.

'I'll go and get a handful of cow cake,' said I.

'Nay, he's quiet eneef.'

The bull went into his stall, the chain which went round his neck lay on the floor, as Percy bent down to pick it up, the bull turned, carrying Percy in front of him into the corner of the four stalled byre.

In the corner were two hay bales, the bull with his head down, pushed Percy between the two bales, it was this that saved him.

The bull was going at him with its big head and the only thing in the small byre was a yard broom. I picked it up, then set about the bull, braying it as hard as ever I possibly could, using it like a hammer on its head and back bone, which seemed to make no impression on the beast.

I thought that it was going to kill the man, then it looked up at me.

It was then I gave it a good stroke across the nose, which made it bleed, luckily for me the bull turned then went back into his stall, and I opened the door to let him go out into he foldyard.

Percy was unable to get up, he was trembling, I was sweating with hitting the bull. I managed to get Percy into the farm house with him leaning on to me. Mrs Corner then rang for the doctor, then the meat company at Aiskew, to come and take the bull away.

Before the wagon came to take the bull away, (he weighed about a ton) Percy felt much better. He had given over trembling though his ribs and left leg hurt him, I sat with him sipping whisky, we were both very lucky. When the wagon came to take the bull away, we walked out to see the two men. 'Now I want that bugger killing before he leaves this farm, I want to see him dead, he could have killed me.'

The bull was put back into his stall, where he was blindfolded, then led out to the wagon where he was shot, then bled, before being winched into the back.

Hope for the best, prepare for the worst.

'It's May Day lads, we'll have yon stirks turned out to grass in the paddock, it's a grand warm day.' May Day being the 13th of May.

Along one side of the paddock ran the overflow out of Johnson's pond. The young stirks were let loose, some ran down the paddock, two ran down the hill, crashing through the hedge into the stell. (gutter).

We ran down to the hedge to find the two stirks up to their necks in puddle, only their heads were showing above the stinking slimy stuff, the stell had been made worse with chaff blowing into it from threshing days over the years.

Ropes were to go for, soon David and Walter came to help us get them out. The stirks were to swill down in Johnson's yard before being taken back to the farm, where they were left out in the foldyard for the day to get used to the strong sunlight.

Stock had built up over the years, especially in cattle, twelve bullocks were gated out at Studley Royal, Ripon. I loved going there with Richard and his dad, to walk round the park looking at their bullocks.

It was a beautiful sunny October day when all the gated-in stock had to be rounded up and taken out of Studley Park, farmers and their men came to round up the bullocks, to drive them into a big pen where they were sorted then loaded into cattle wagons. Richard and I set off to walk to the far side of the park, the trees were in their autumn colours, underneath the chestnut trees lay lots of conkers, herds of deer were resting under some of them, the stags were busy running about. Some were not to be trusted, one came for Richard and me, it was just as well we carried good strong sticks to defend ourselves.

All the bullocks gated out had to be de-horned; to mark his stock, Percy had P.C. burnt into the front hoofs of each bullock.

While we were sorting them out another farmer claimed one of ours as his own, he had to back down when shown the initials burnt into the hoof.

Back home the bullocks were put into a good fog field, but when we looked round them the next morning the best bullock was missing. After a full search of the surrounding fields we were unable to find it so the police were informed of the missing beast. We never did find the missing bullock.

He that spends well needs no account book.

Percy had bought a combine harvester and after harvest the straw bales were stacked out in the fields, which made more room in the Dutch barn for other things, such as lambing pens and a bay for storing the potatoes, this made it better for riddling when under cover.

It was while we were busy riddling potatoes that a car came into the yard, one of many with the farm being near the road to Crakehall, probably the representative wanted a quick sale.

'Keep on riddling, lads, make him wait a bit, then he'll probably go away,' said Percy. The young chap got out of the car looking starved to death. He stood looking at us wondering what to do, eventually the riddle stopped.

'Now young man, what are you looking for, 'NIGHT' you'll not find it here. Have you got out of bed on the wrong side this morning? You don't look ower pleased with thee sen, what's ter selling?'

Rep: 'Fire extinguishers.'

'We have no use for them here, we can't afford to be lighting fires just ti sit ower an keep warm, we have to work here to do that, good day.'

After the heavy snow fall of 1963 came the gale force wind, which came on a Sunday night sweeping down off Johnson's Piney Moor field to give the four Council houses which stood on high ground a good battering. Charlie Catterick and I were out early morning with flashlights looking at the roof to see if any tiles had been blown off.

All the tiles seemed to be lifted up at the same time, then dropped back down again. The gale force wind returned again on the Monday night, some gusts would be up to a hundred miles an hour.

Tuesday morning when Richard and I fed the pigs outside, the steel bin which would hold five hundredweight of pig nuts was missing. While looking for the bin we came across a corrugated tin sheet embedded into a wooden gate post, we never did find the missing bin.

Trees were blown down in thousands, the park at Jervaulx looked as if woodmen had felled all the trees.

Better to give a shilling than lend half a crown.

'There's a tup sale at Hawes today lads, we'll gan up yonder, I want three cheap Swaledale tups if possible. We'll ev dinner at Mrs D'Lacey's seeing as we will be in Hawes, we'll tak a good lowance with us.'

Richard driving, Percy and I sat in the front of the Land Rover, taking the cattle trailer with us we set off for Hawes.

On the way up we saw what other farmers were doing on the land, who farmed which land, what condition their stock was in. At the mart, Percy had a word for every one, such as, 'Thoo looks grumpy this morning, wats thoo had for breakfast, cold shoulder and tongue?'

Kit Calvert, a well-known local was always about the Auction Mart. Old Kit smoked a clay pipe, he was good to get along with.

The three tups were bought and loaded into the cattle trailer. 'When we get up yonder, we'll have 'em branded before we let 'em loose, then a rough count of the sheep on't low land, but before we go we'll ev dinner.'

The three tups were ear-punched with Corner's mark, then let go among the ewes. Later, when the sheep were gathered up, one tup was missing.

'Aye why, it's what you can expect at this time of year, they will have been fighting, yan on 'em will have killed it.'

We never did find that tup that winter.

Snaizeholme in spring is a lovely place to be, with only the birds' song to break the silence. Our first task when arriving at the farm was to light the kitchen fire, to warm the house. After having a good lowance

Richard and I set off to make our way onto the fell top, Capp the young dog went with us, while old Bob stayed with Percy.

As we made our way to the boundary wall, peewits wheeled about protecting their nests, redshanks flew about, as we climbed higher curlews were disturbed from nesting. When we reached the boundary wall we came across a 'thirl-hole' or 'cripple-ole' as we called them.

This is a hole made in the wall for sheep to pass through into another field. This one had pig netting in front instead of the usual board to stop it up. Here was the missing tup, the skull and horns still hanging on the wire where it had been caught.

Its bones lay on the ground picked clean by carrion crows and foxes.

A fool may give a wise man counsel.

A shed was built on the fell-side at Snaizeholme for the sheep and beasts to shelter in. The three bay barn which had a tin roof and sides, had to be inspected by the man from the Ministry at Northallerton.

'Reet lads, we'll go up yonder and play about till he's been.'

Out on the fell-side stood the brand new shed, well built by a firm from Hawes. We walked over to it with the Ministry man who had a good look at it and said, 'It should have been put up level, not following the slope of the land.'

Percy: 'Nay be buggered, if it had gone up level, the stock would have been able to walk onto the roof, then what?'

Ministry man: 'Fence it round and put a gate on.'

Percy: 'Don't talk so bloody daft, what are you getting paid for? How will the stock get in for shelter?'

Min. Man: 'Well I can't pass it for subsidy until you paint it green.'

Percy: 'Out else rang wi it, and what sort of green do you want it painting, ez green ez you are?'

The shed was painted green. 'I'll remember him, the little Hitler.'

Sixty ewes were on the farm at Snaizeholme when Percy took it over, he was only able to claim subsidy on sixty out of the 300 on the farm. 'Reet lads, we'll gan up yonder this morning, Ministry man is coming to have a look at yon yows which get Government Subsidy, we'll gan an play about till he's gone.'

Playing about meant walling up gaps. We were busy walling when a man came into sight, he must have walked a mile, leaving his car well down the lane. When he came near, we could see that he was the same man who had come to inspect the barn.

'Let him come to us, it will do him good to walk,' said Percy.

'I've come to inspect the ewes that get subsidy, you can only claim on sixty,' said he.

Percy looking up onto the fell top, and seeing some sheep on the sky line, said, 'Them's them, reet on t' top, I've just bowt these here on t' low land.'

Then away the man set off to walk onto the fell top.

'Let him go, ar'll get me own back now, the little Hitler as he is.'

Soon as the man went out of sight we set off for home.

The poor man's shilling is but a penny.

It was a Saturday afternoon in November, one of those days when fog hung about. Old Joe Pratt, the village poacher, was missing.

Old Joe had had his left hand amputated as a young man, after a horse had bitten it. It was around 5 o'clock when word came round that Joe was missing. George Smith, John Horner, Fred Atkinson and I walked over to the ghyll, shouting as we walked the full length of it. Carrying stable lamps, we resumed our search after tea, by then the fog was much thicker. It was only by chance that we walked over to where some trees had been felled and pulled out of the ghyll and came across old Joe grumbling aloud to himself about getting out of the wood.

He never answered our calling, he had walked astride a thin tree until he came to where one tree was on top of the other and he could go no further. He didn't have the sense to walk backwards. We had to go for a chair to carry him home – not forgetting the pheasant he had shot.

Fred, who lived in Burrill, worked for Coldicott and each Saturday night Fred and I went to visit his parents who lived at Hornby Castle, then to the pub at Hackforth. One Saturday night a farmer's son came rushing in, asking for volunteers to kill rats, a swarm had come on to the farm at Tunstall, near Catterick. The pub soon emptied, Fred taking a van load, others from Hackforth came, bringing their terrier dogs.

When we arrived at the farm the buildings were overrun with rats.

It was a bit scary seeing so many rats running around. The farm had no electric light, stable lamps and torches were used, some dogs were bitten very badly, one had to have a rat killed while still clinging to its mouth.

On the Sunday morning Fred and I went back to the farm, they had gathered up 73 dead rats, all the others had moved away.

The boughs that bear the most hang the lowest.

A tree in a 'sink hole' stood on the lower ground at Snaizeholme. The round hole would be some 50 feet across, the tree 25 feet or so tall. One winter, after a fall of snow, the wind continued to blow, filling the hole level with packed snow, leaving the top thin branches showing. The sheep came along and gnarled the bark off until the branches were white, when the snow melted the top of the tree showed up very white. When anyone came for a look round the farm and came across the tree they would say 'Look at that tree, why is like that?' When we replied, 'Oh, that, the sheep have eaten it off,' they then looked at you as though you were a fool. As Percy once said, 'Our sheep can climb trees when they are hungry, and so would you if you were hungry.'

It was while walking along the fell-side and talking about things in general that Percy said to me, 'The way things are going today, it will soon be all dog and stick as we are doing now, the least productive will get the most money.' He was referring to those in professional sport.

He also posed this question:

A farmer had three sons and 17 cows.
The eldest son had to have half the cows,
The next son had to have one third of them,
The youngest son to have one ninth of the cows.

How does he do it?

Three men book a room for the day in an Hotel,
The porter says £10 each – £30

The owner says he has charged them £5 too much and tells him give them it back. The porter puts two pounds in his pocket, then gives each man a pound back, so each man has now paid £9. 3 x £9 = £27, £2 in the porter's pocket = £29. Where has the other pound gone?

An English summer, three hot days and a thunderstorm.

After one thunderstorm when we looked round the stock at Snaizeholme we found a dead cow which had been struck by lightning.

After the vet had inspected the cow, it had to be buried where it lay. The man who picked up fallen stock was unable to remove the carcase because it was in such an out of way place. Percy and I went the following morning to bury the cow.

'We'll soon have the job done before the walkers come to complain about it.' said Percy. (Fell walkers were coming out more at weekends, Dodd Fell was an attraction for them, because of the old Roman road which went across into Wharfedale.) When digging, we soon struck rock, it took all day to get a hole deep enough to bury the cow. Travelling up the next morning, Percy said, 'We'll soon eft job hap't up this morning.'

It had rained overnight up there and the hole was full of water. Percy and I pushed the dead cow into the hole, it hit the water, then turned over on to its back with its legs up in the air. 'Well, that's a bugger, arl let wind out of her with me knife to see if that will sink her,' said Percy, rubbing the blade up and down his leather leggings to sharpen it. Percy did his best to let the wind out of the dead cow. It would not sink, there was only one way, we had to dig a trench to let the water out, even then the dead cow's legs were to break to get it to the bottom of the hole, to get it well covered up. It was night when we arrived back at Cowling. As I left the farm to go home Percy said, 'An deean't tell Walter it's ta'en two days to bury a cow or we'll never hear the end of it.'

To drive from the farm buildings at Snaizeholme, a very steep hill had to be negotiated; the Land Rover wheels used to spin, sending stones flying down the hill. Percy had the hill cemented, with grooves made in it for a better grip and to channel the water off the hill.

In late October, the cows with calves were to be taken back to the

Home Farm at Cowling for the winter months. A cattle wagon managed to get down to the farm buildings. Six cows with calves were loaded but when the wagon set off up the hill, the front wheels lifted off the ground and half-way up, the wagon began to come backwards down the hill.

'Right lads, grab some big stones,' shouted Percy, 'and be ready to scotch the back wheels.' When the front wheels touched the ground, Richard and I managed to get the big stones behind the wheels to hold the wagon. If it had gone over the grass, it would have gone down a hill into a beck. Luckily no cows were injured. A tractor from another farm had to help pull the empty wagon up the hill onto the lane.

A pen had to be made in the lane for loading sheep and beasts, which took quite a while, as everything for making it had to be taken up from the Home Farm.

A fool may ask more questions in an hour than a wise man can answer.

Percy and I had been weighing bacon pigs in the top yard when, walking back to the farm, we saw Walter Johnson outside his barn door, brush in hand. Walter was always sweeping up.

'We'll gan and have a word wi Walter an see what he ez ti say.'

We were busy putting the world to rights when a Rover car came slowly round the corner then stopped, the driver asking the way to Leyburn.

'LEYBURN?' said Percy, I knew then what to expect. 'It's a lang way frev here, we don't gan far from home, we can't afford it, the've gitten th sen's lost, Walter.'

'Which road do we take?' asked the driver.

'You don't tak onny, you leave the road where it is, we want to use it this efterneean, come all the way frev Leeds, just ti get thee sen lost.'

'We are from Staffordshire,' replied the young woman next to the driver.

'By, that's a lang way ti cu fra just ti get thee sen lost.'

Then Walter suggested, 'It wad be better if he could reverse that flash car, then gan up t' old lane here, there's nobbut three yats ti oppen, that way he wad be gahin ti Leyburn, he could allus call on Stan Trewhitt an ask him the way, he rides about on a bike, I know he gans a lang way frev yam, Dennis here comes from up that way.

'That's thee best road, strait on till yer come ti't main road, then turn left, you can tak that road ti Leyburn, we don't use it.'

'How far is that?' asked the driver?'

'I deean't know, we don't gan far from here,' said Percy.

After the car had gone, Walter smiling said, 'That cap't him, they think we are all thick up here, so we might as well act like it, what do you say Percy?'

'Caps me where they get all t'brass from to buy big cars, just to ride around our countryside an do nowt, you and I are in the wrong business, Walter.'

He who does not rise early, never does a good day's work.

'You will all come in good time in the morning, then we'll get done in good time,' said Percy. The morning being Christmas Day.

It was snowing when George Smith and I set off to walk to the farm at 5.45 for a 6 o'clock start. Old Joe was busy feeding the pigs when we arrived. It was while Percy and I were chopping turnips that the electricity went off. Stable lamps were lit, it was snowing faster. 'I've rang the lectric at Bedale, a man will be here in half an hour.'

The electric man came and located the fault, it was the lead-in cable which went into the buildings above the barn door where old Bob the farm dog stayed. The repair man was putting the ladder up when Bob nipped him, on the leg.

'That's it,' shouted the man, 'you can get someone else to do that job!'

'No, don't be like that how-ay in and have some breakfast wi us, an lets ev a leeak at wot 'es deean ti thee leg, I'm sure if he'd bit thee leg thee right arm would have been missing, we'll all gan in for breakfast, how-ay in.'

The nip was very little, fright being the worst problem. It was still snowing fast at breakfast. 'After breakfast we'll have the sheep racks out and filled with good hay, then ta'en into the pasture whilst waiting for t' lectric to be put reet. We'll feed the hens, and all the outside stock, give em a double do this morning, then we'll get back home, it won tak lang.'

We had to wait for daylight before going round the outside stock and taking the sheep racks out, arriving home in time for Christmas dinner.

No more they hear the rising of the lark from the dewy grass,
Nor the tuneful thrush from the hedge that sings,
Nor the blackbirds that welcome spring from the highest bough,
Their work is done, their eyes dim with death,
No more a Pilgrim here on earth . . .

The end of January 1966, I left Percy and moved from Burrill to Marton, near Middlesbrough. Our eldest son, Michael, would soon be fourteen years old and we wanted our two sons to have a better chance in life than I had.

Marton took a lot of getting used to, no one had the time to stop and speak. After village life it seemed awful not being spoken to.

Tom Ellis farmed nearby, they were the first to invite us to their house for tea. Today they live at Northallerton, moving there when their farm was taken over for building on. Where Tom's cattle grazed, there now stands a shopping centre, it took preference over farm stock. The fields that I ploughed and drilled with corn for Jim Alderson are covered with houses and a school.

Once in summer time we had swallows flying about, at dusk bats flitted around; now with the farm buildings being obliterated to build Hemlington and Coulby Newham housing estates, we have none.

The cuckoo no longer calls out, the swift is non-existent, footpaths made in woods near where I live enable those with air guns easy access to take pot shots at small birds. Yet the authorities claim to be doing so much in the name of conservation of wild life.

The first night out I had after leaving Burrill was with our next door neighbour Dick Richardson, he took me to the Highfield Hotel.

There was none of the usual 'Woryerevein?' Looking round, I saw a table with an old gentleman sitting all alone. As I walked over to him he gave me a smile, then as soon as I spoke to him said, 'You are not from round here, sit down and talk to me, all they talk about here is pig iron and football. I'm from Richmond, it sounds as if you are from the same place.' He told me that he was a Brown from Downholme, the transport people, that he had helped to start the business with his father, using horses and carts. The old gentleman was so pleased he had someone to talk to in his dialect, he asked Dick and me to his home to meet his wife. I went a second time then sadly, not long after, he passed away.

The death of wolves is the safety of the sheep.

It was while working for Jim Alderson, that I saw the worst sheep worrying while working on the farms.

It was dark when I arrived for work one February morning in 1971. I went to see Jim in the cow byre, he told me, 'We have had the dogs among the sheep, I have seen one dead, when it's daylight, you and I will have a better look.'

Daylight came, we walked to the field where the flock of ewes with their lambs were, it was like a battlefield.

Out of his flock of 70 Clun ewes, 36 lay dead or had to be destroyed. Lambs which had been born at Christmas, lay dead. One lamb I well remember had its stomach hanging out and stood bleating for its mother which lay dead. Wool torn off the sheep lay like snow on the field, sheep which had survived the onslaught were to find in other fields, some were still fast in the hedges where they had tried to escape from the dogs.

End of September that year I left Jim, his farm had been sold for building on. October, I started work for Middlesbrough Council. When working on the farms I was given this advice. 'You want nowt working with a lot of men, it will be all argument and fighting.'

This was on my mind when I started work for Middlesbrough Council but during the eighteen years that I worked for the Parks Department I never witnessed any fighting or listened to a serious argument.

My first day at Stewart Park I well remember. After signing my name in the book, I was told to, 'Just wait there, go and see John in the tractor garage.'

John Harvey was the head mechanic in charge of all the tractors. To my surprise he had lived at Masham, going to school there. I asked John why all the waiting. 'The cutters you want for that tractor are being repaired by the mechanics round in the back yard.'

'Just wait there' came to 12 o'clock, a young man, Kenny Holmes ,was the first one to call in at the garage, his cutters had broken. 'You are coming with me this afternoon, I'll keep you right, when we go round to the mechanic's shop, don't pick up any spanners to do the job yourself, they don't like you doing their work. Some are strong Union men, it could cause a strike., it seems the less you know here, the better you get on.' 'Just wait there' lasted until after 2 o'clock. One hour cutting grass on a playing field completed my first day at work.

Teesside had been formed when I started work at Stewart Park, where a work force of 65 signed in each morning. They included painters, joiners, mechanics, greenhouse staff, van drivers, park keepers, tractor drivers and others. My first summer I had the task of cutting the grass along the roadsides using a Banks Master, which had a seven yard reach. I started near Redcar and went to Eston where the machine was garaged each night, then to Billingham and Stockton, where I came in contact with other council workers.

John Harvey came each day with fuel and to check the machine over. I was taken in the van to be shown the easy way through Stockton starting at the far side of the town. It was while I was cutting a bank in Stockton, that a young school boy came past. I had picked the cutting head up when he walked underneath putting his arm up to touch the cutters. Lucky for me the cutting head was out of his reach.

At Thornaby I had a lot of trouble with the children when cutting near Council houses. It was here, when the machine was garaged at Little Boy Park, that thieves broke in and stole all the tools out of the tractor.

During winter months the tractor drivers were put on stand-by, you were on call any time during the night, and weekends.

Snow ploughs were fitted to all the tractors, two tractors worked together. Dick Turnbull and I were together clearing the roads at Nunthorpe once in the early hours of the morning. a man stood in the middle of the road waving his arms, 'Come quickly, my wife is trapped between the car and the garage door.' With the chains which we carried we were able to pull the car back up the icy slope and free his wife. She had got out of the car to lift the garage door up when the car slid forward trapping her.

We were not always angels. A strong east wind was causing drifting on the Stokesley-Nunthorpe stretch of road, four snow-ploughs were working through the night to keep it open. A car came past travelling to Middlesbrough then got fast in the snow. If he had followed the ploughs to Poole roundabout he would have been able to travel. It was follow my leader. When I saw the tractor in front push snow up to the car, I did the same, and the other two.

A meeting took place at the roundabout, it was decided we would go to the boundary line, then stop on our return to ask if he wanted pulling out, but only if he put the chain on his car, then took it off.

In heavy snow falls the first priority was that the main bus routes had to be clear of snow, also roads to and round hospitals.

Car parks were cleared of snow during the night, all cars were supposed to have been taken out. The snow had to be pushed one way, any cars left in overnight had snow pushed up to them so that next time they would move them.

The big council estates were next. Kenny Holmes and I were working together and he gave me this advice, 'Never stop, keep going, follow me.'

I soon found out why, gangs of youths had snowballs ready, the tractors were pelted with them, more than the windscreen wipers could cope with. Some householders had cleared the path, putting the snow on the road. As I followed Ken, I was pushing the snow back onto the path, spades and shovels were thrown at the tractor. To overcome this we left the estate for the country roads, returning early morning to waken them up. Helping one another, four tractors cleared the road in one sweep, we also made plenty of noise.

A beggar can never be bankrupt.

Hemlington had sixteen men sitting down in the mess room for a midday break and it was here that I got an eye opener. It was pay day, the security van called around midday. Most of the workers were young, single men. I had never seen anything like it before, when they opened their pay packets: 'You owe me two pounds.' 'I lent you three pounds a week ago.' 'I gave you it back.' 'I owe you four pounds.' I remember one young man borrowing the next day, he had paid back nearly all his wages.

The poor man's table is soon spread.

It was at Hemlington when they came in for dinner that I noticed a lot of them were carrying a tin of Coke and a packet of crisps. This was their midday meal. I asked them why they did not bring sandwiches the same as I did, you can't work on that. 'We aren't farm workers like you tractor men, I couldn't eat fat bacon in a sandwich, we can't afford boots like you.' Some only had sandshoes on their feet. I was always taught when on the farms, 'Good grub and good working clothes kept a man at work.'

A moneyless man goes fast through the market.

Unions had never bothered me, I had got along very well without them but I had to join to be like the rest of them. In January 1979 the Council binmen in London were on strike for more pay. Into the tractor garage came a Union man. 'Will you support our brothers in London, give a pound a week?' At that time there were fifteen tractor drivers, all ex-farm workers like myself. Two weeks later the Union man returned bringing with him a top man from Newcastle, demanding money for our brothers in London. I was told that if I did not pay the £3 I would have a black mark put against my name, if I left my job they would see that I never got another.

What did Mammy's little boy do.

When Teesside became Cleveland County I only had the roadside grass in the Middlesbrough area to cut with the Banks Master.

I had to cut grass on the estates, parks and playing fields until the wild flowers had seeded. When the schools were closed for the summer holidays, the little devils came in hordes to where you were cutting grass with the tractor and seven gang. They would ride on the cutters, their toes one inch from the revolving blades.

Nails and bits of iron were pushed into the path of the cutters, tin cans were thrown at the cutters to try and stop you, stones were thrown at the tractor, windows were broken. You dared not leave the tractor standing alone or there would be a flat tyre, the valve taken out.

When cutting on Thorntree Estate Kenny Holmes did have a child in the cutters dragging him along, his legs and arms were cut, the ambulance took him to hospital. The mothers who stood outside watching blamed the driver, not the child.

The Council were putting a marquee up for a children's party at St Hilda's, what we called 'Over the border'. Six men had been trying to pull the marquee up, but were unable to with all the children on it.

I was cutting Albert Park when they came and asked if I would go and pull it up with the tractor, keeping the children away, I pulled it up. Before I left the little devils had got onto the top of the marquee and were sliding down the canvas holding onto a knife, cutting it as they came down, the marquee was then taken down.

The more farm land the Council took over for the building of houses the more we had to cut for hay. Acres of hay were set on fire. The kids carried the hay off at night to make a shelter to play in, usually covering a bush over with it. Two fields we cut at Acklam had a beck running full length along them. They dammed the beck up with hay. When we were baling they carried the bales away. When asked what they were going to do with it, they replied, 'Mary 'as a pony to feed and she wants some hay for it.' When baling and leading the bales out of Saltersgill playing field, the little devils cut most of the bands on the bales, because they could not have a ride on the trailer. One year a young girl broke her arm jumping off a load of bales and a boy got his foot fast in the rope and was dragged along.

Puddle Ombrometer

I was loading rubbish which had been gathered up from around the estate, out of flower beds etc. because wet days meant the tractor drivers leading rubbish to the tip at Seal Sands, Billingham. Going into Beechwood cabin for midday break, where all the men were sat, I heard one of them who was looking out of the window declare, 'It's too wet to go out,' I asked him how he knew this when looking on to the tool shed. 'Oh, we have a puddle ombrometer, have a look.' They had a hole in the ground lined with plastic, about a foot across filled with water. 'If we can count twelve rings on that it's too wet to go out.'

What's only an inconvenience to one is starvation to another.

You may think that cutting grass on a Housing Estate was easy. The grass belongs to different departments. On the daily work sheet it would look like this:

Housing 17/03 Open space - 17/01   Main Road 15/11
2 hours.   1 hour 10 mins.   3 hours
Other roads: 15/31.-   1 hour 30 mins.
Travelling time: 20 mins.   8 hours.

No sooner had we got used to the numbers when they were changed.

Perhaps someone sitting behind a desk wanted a job. When working with the woodman, the tree had a number e.g. Tree D664/64 and when the tree was cut into sections for loading, tree sections D002/37.

Time and Motion Study.

I was cutting the banks along Stokesley road when a young man came carrying a board and stop watch. 'I have come to time you cutting the banks for bonus, the more you do the more bonus you will get.'

First I had to cut where there were obstacles, trees, signposts etc. When cutting up the cam-side I reached the top with only half the cutting head in use. He tapped on the side window. 'It's only cutting half the width of the cutter.'

'Yes, I know, if you can tell me how I can bend the cutting head to cut the flat I will gladly do so.'

'Oh, I never thought of that.'

Makes you wonder.

In the afternoon I had to cut where there were no obstacles so I asked him if he wanted a ride inside the cab because once it started it would never stop unless some unseen wire got round the cutting blades. No, he would walk behind to do his job properly. There came a thunder storm and he got wet through.

It's better to be wise than foolish

West Beck had to be cleaned out. Bill Bray, the senior foreman was in charge, woodmen were taking some branches off trees, felling others, some men were taking the rubbish out of the beck, throwing it out on to the grass to be picked up and taken to the tip. I was using the loader with the winch behind for winching the tree trunks out of the beck.

Arriving on the job the next morning, we found the beck had been dammed up with the rubbish which had been thrown out the day before.

Around mid morning three youths came along, they started to throw some more rubbish back into the beck. Bill Bray, a big strong man gave them a warning, 'Give over, or you will be in the beck.' All he got was a lot of cheek. They were standing where the water was deep near the dam. Bill walked over to them casually lighting a cigarette, the largest one he pushed into the water, then grabbed hold of the other two, lifted them up – one in each hand – then threw them into the water.

A fire had to be lit each day to burn the wood, using the loader with a chain and the tree dogs to pick the big pieces up to carry to the fire. I had a young man putting the tree dogs on, he told me he was an Italian Jew. The problem was that after putting the tree dogs on the limb, he would stand in front of the log. I told him about this, that I could not stop the log from swinging when lifted. I reported it to the supervisor to protect myself in case of an accident.

Came the day when he put the tree dogs on, I gave the trunk a lift off the ground and he walked in front of it. The swinging log caught him in the back, knocking him to the ground. Resting the log on the ground, I went to him to see what damage had been done or if there were any broken bones. It is surprising how you can remember things, especially swear words. I told him off in English, using Italian words mixed in, he got the message. 'I'm all right,' he said, then asked if I had been a prisoner of war. Bill Bray sent him home to rest or perhaps to get him out of the way.

See listen and be silent, and you will live in peace.

Hemlington Hall Farm had been taken over by Middlesbrough Council.

Two rockeries had to be made on the hillside facing the lake.

The big stones would weigh over a ton each, my job was lifting the stones into place, using a chain on the loader. The stones were to let into the ground. By 10 o'clock the charge hand and his men had two large stones in place. Along came the foreman onto the job, looking at the two stones he said, 'They're no good like that, I want them taking out and putting the other way round, they will look much better.'

By midday the stones had been taken out and turned round. It was just after one o'clock when the supervisor came, 'What the hell do you call this? They ought to be the other way round, fancy putting them in like that.' The two stones were taken out and turned round. While we were doing this the Parks manager came, 'Who told you to put them like that? I'm sure they would look better the other way round.'

The two stones eventually ended up the same way as Brian the charge hand had put them!

Better to say here it is, than here it was.

'This morning Den, go and load rubbish at Pallister Park, you will have three trailers and two wagons today.' So said Norman, the foreman. When I arrived at the Park the police were there. When I asked the Parks foreman why, he said, 'VANDALISM! Go and have a look.'

The tiles had been taken off the roof to the Ladies and Gents toilets to gain entry, everything inside the toilets was broken, water was running out of them, flower beds had been desecrated, seats broken, holes made in the bowling greens, a hole made in the roof of the Club house, cups etc. smashed on the floor, windows broken.

I had heard of vandalism, this was the first time I had seen it. It was heart breaking to see to much unwanted damage done.

And nothing came out of the bag but what was put in it.

We now have a Leisure Farm, though what leisure there is on a farm I do not know. Before it was opened I had to rotovate the land between the cart track and a wall, about 150 yards long by 4 yards wide, which the public were expected to use. Norman Lane, the tractor foreman, came to see me in the works van. 'I've brought you some wild flower seeds to put on Den, they have come from Poland. Don't waste them, what's in that bag cost £70. The public will like to see a few wild flowers when walking down here, make sure they are spread full length after you have put the grass seed on.' Grass will grow in a low temperature. The day before the Leisure Farm was to be opened I was told, 'Right, Den, you put a bandit on, go up to the Leisure Farm and you know that wall you drilled the grass seed behind – go and cut it.'

'What about the wild flowers the public wanted to see?'

'We are not here to reason why, go and cut it!'

It's better to enjoy the bright days than brood over t'darkuns.

When at Burrill, rush hour for me used to be two tractors and a car. I had put a load of coke on to a trailer for the greenhouses in Albert Park, Ken Horner was taking it. I was following on behind with the loader to push the coke under cover. It was early morning rush hour, cars came between Ken and me going towards the traffic lights on Marton Road. He had forgotten to put his tipping gear out of action and the load of coke went out of the trailer on to the road, cars were going left and right. The coke was taken off the road in record time before the police came along.

'Before you go to load soil this morning, Den, put a load of coke on for Kenny Holmes, it's for Age Croft. You will have five trailers leading soil today.' The next morning I was told, 'Before you go to load soil, go to Age Croft and put that load of coke under cover, I forgot to give Kenny the key.' When I arrived at Age Croft I thought that someone must have put the coke under cover by hand.

Opening the door I found the place was empty, the load of coke had been stolen.

A dry May and a dripping June, brings all things into tune.

'You never baled yon hay yesterday, Dennis,' said the Parks Manager.

'It was never fit to bale,' said I.

'We were at York yesterday, they were baling down there.'

'Maybe so, York isn't up here.'

'You put the turner on, Den,' said Norman the tractor foreman, 'then go and start to turn yon hay, they want it baling.'

'It's not fit to bale yet Norman.'

'I know that, *you* know that, do *they* know that?'

It was a Scotch mist that morning when I left Stewart Park for the Leisure Farm where a pasture had been cut for hay, it was lush and very green when cut, the hay turned like rope.

I had been twice round the field when Bill Bentley came into the field with the baler, by then it was nearly raining.

When I was giving Bill a hand to open the baler out I said, 'Surely you are not going to start baling, Bill?'

'Yes I am, they have sent the right man this time.' Two men were leaning over the gate to watch Bill start baling.

The afternoon was sunny and hot, had the hay been left it would have baled lovely.

That night a gang of men went to lead the bales, they refused to lift them, they were far too heavy for them to handle.

The farmer and his cows.

He borrows one from his neighbour to make eighteen.

One half	9
One third	6
One ninth	2
	17

Then he takes the farmer his cow back.

I'll lap up now and call it night.

111

Some dialect words.

a'e' ti	-	have to
a'e' ti ev	-	have to have
allus	-	always
an't	-	and the
ar'd	-	I had
arl	-	I will
arn	-	earn
ar's	-	I am
beeath	-	both
beeats	-	boots
billy band	-	string
breckus	-	breakfast
brout	-	brought
choch	-	church
coo	-	cow
dee	-	do
deean	-	done
deean't	-	don't
duzter	-	do you
ed	-	had
'eeard	-	heard
ee's	-	eyes
eft	-	have it
eneeaf	-	enough
etta	-	have to
ez	-	as
ezent	-	has not

fost	-	first
fo't	-	for the
fra, frev	-	from
gan	-	go
gat	-	got
gihan	-	going
hissen	-	himself
hug	-	carry
lang	-	long
larl	-	little
leeaks	-	looks
lig	-	lay
lowance	-	snack
lowse	-	loose
mich	-	much
mun	-	must
nay	-	no
neet	-	night
nivver	-	never
onny	-	any
orth	-	earth
ower	-	over
plooin	-	ploughing
sa	-	so
sec, sek	-	sack
seean	-	soon
see'd	-	saw

ta' en't	-	taken it
tahm	-	time
team	-	to empty
teeak	-	took
thoo'll	-	you will
thoo's	-	you are
ti', tiv	-	to
ti' ev	-	to have
ti' how	-	to hoe
ti't	-	to the
wad	-	would
we'em	-	with them
we'ent	-	will not, wont
wi	-	with
yakker	-	acre
yam	-	home
yance	-	once
yer'll	-	you will
yer'll etta	-	you'll have to
yows	-	ewes